Pro-Choice/Pro-Life, *Let's Work Together*

Reducing Unplanned Pregnancies to
Reduce Stress on Women and Reduce Abortions

Wayne Van Der Wal, Ed.S.

Table of Contents

**"Truth does not mind being questioned.
A lie does not like being challenged."
~unknown**

In this book, I seek to share truth and foster unity. But truth isn't always comfortable—it can challenge us, forcing us to confront ourselves in ways we may not like.

Though truth can be painful, embracing it with humility can free us from the games we play and the burdens we carry.

I invite you to read with an open mind. Whether you agree or not, I hope you'll gain a new perspective.

Thank you for taking the time to share this journey with me—it truly means a lot. 😊

Wayne
Wayne Van Der Wal, Ed.S.
School psychologist, counselor, life coach

Chapter 1

The Why: Why this book?

pro-choice (adjective): favoring the legalization of abortion (Merriam-Webster)

Mary

"I was 18 at the end of high school when I discovered I was pregnant. I grew up with a hardworking single mom of three, and as the oldest, I felt immense pressure. The man involved had just become my ex—a 21-year-old college junior with the maturity of a 15-year-old, still living off his parents and known for his womanizing and controlling behavior.

I kept the pregnancy a secret to shield my already-overburdened mom and to avoid any lasting connection with him. Although I had always dreamed of having children and a family, I wasn't ready—emotionally, mentally, or financially—to raise a child on my own. Abortion seemed like my only option. The clinic treated the procedure as routine, so I didn't think of it as anything major. When I returned home, I simply told my mom I had the flu..."

(Continued in Chapter 8)

pro-life (adjective): opposed to abortion

Josiah

"In 1995, a woman in South Korea became pregnant while living with her partner. They already had a daughter and were struggling financially, so she decided to have an abortion at two months. The procedure—a curettage abortion—was meant to remove the baby in pieces. However, at five months, she realized the abortion had failed, and the baby was still growing.

At that point, the family chose adoption. On October 7, 1995, the baby—me—was born. I was healthy except for a deformed arm. I lived in a foster home until I was 13 months old, when I was adopted by a loving family in Norman, Oklahoma..."
(Continued in Chapter 9)

Why do I want Pro-Choice and Pro-Life people to work together?

My primary goal in writing this book is to eliminate unplanned pregnancies for two reasons. First, reducing the number of unintended pregnancies would alleviate the stress and difficult decisions women face in such situations. **Second**, without unplanned pregnancies, there would be no abortions—and no debates over abortion. Wouldn't that be nice? While I may not see this reality in my lifetime, this book aims to reduce the number of abortions.

To achieve this goal of reducing unplanned pregnancies—and therefore reducing stress on women and the number of abortions—I believe we are stronger *together* than we are divided. In my experience having personally been both pro-choice and pro-life, and knowing and counseling innumerable women from both the pro-choice and pro-life sides, I've seen that most people agree on the importance of reducing unplanned pregnancies. I believe this is something about which most, if not all, of us can agree. When we're united, I know we can make a difference.

Our goal is to reduce unplanned pregnancies to reduce stress on women and reduce abortions. We can do this together!

Part 1

Healthy Dialogue for
Finding Common Ground

Chapter 2

Three Needs for Working Together

Active Listening, Empathy, and Clear Definitions

As an adult—both in my personal life and as a school psychologist, counselor, and life coach—I've observed that many conflicts remain unresolved because people talk (or yell) at each other instead of truly listening. Active listening is essential for productive conversations.

Without active listening, empathy is impossible. Empathy means putting yourself in someone else's shoes, seeing their perspective, and understanding their thoughts and feelings. It reminds us the other person is human, with experiences worth valuing and learning from. Empathy is key to working together.

Another common reason arguments go nowhere is miscommunication. People may use the same words but define them differently. As a result, they aren't even debating the same thing, which leads to endless back and forth without resolution. To move forward, we need to agree on clear definitions.

For any disagreement to be productive, both sides must be willing to find common ground. This requires:

1. **Active listening**
2. **Empathy**
3. **Clear, shared definitions**

Practicing these skills strengthens ALL relationships—whether with family, friends, coworkers, or people who have opposing beliefs. If we commit to using active listening, empathy, and clear definitions, we can build better understanding and stronger connections.

Why Discuss These Three Needs?

Abortion is one of the most controversial and emotionally charged topics today. But instead of real debate, I see constant clashes—name-calling, yelling, lying, exaggerating, changing the subject, suppressing free speech, interrupting, and a win-or-lose mindset instead of a solution-focused, win-win approach.

Because of this ongoing hostility between pro-choice and pro-life advocates, I believe it's important to set a healthier tone for those willing to engage in thoughtful discussion.

As you read this book, you may come across ideas you dislike or disagree with. But I encourage you to practice active listening (reading) and empathy and accept neutral, third-party definitions. By doing so, you might discover you have more in common with your "opponent" than you thought.

So, are you willing to find common ground with those who disagree with you on abortion?

If so, keep reading. If not, keep reading. Maybe something you read will make you willing!

Our goal is to reduce unplanned pregnancies to reduce stress on women and reduce abortions. We can do this together!

"Coming together is the beginning.
Keeping together is progress.
Working together is success."
~Henry Ford

"Alone we can do so little; together we can do so much."
~unknown

"We all do better when we work together. Our differences do matter, but our common humanity matters more."
~Bill Clinton

Chapter 3

Active Listening

(Note: This is not a counseling manual. Chapters 3 and 4 introduce conflict-resolution techniques to help us approach this challenging topic with an open and healthy mindset. These skills can improve ALL of your relationships.)

Active listening is more than just hearing words—it's about fully understanding the speaker's meaning, emotions, and intent.

Key Strategies for Active Listening:
- **Check your mindset:** Let go of personal biases and judgments. Take a deep breath and remind yourself that you're there to understand, not to "win."
- **Be fully present:** Maintain eye contact, use open body language, and create a safe, respectful space for honest conversation.
- **Read emotions and cues:** Pay attention to facial expressions, tone of voice, and body language. Acknowledge the speaker's feelings before responding.
- **Listen to understand:** Focus on what the speaker is saying instead of planning your reply. Allow them to finish without interrupting.

- **Paraphrase and clarify:** Restate important points in your own words—for example, "So you're saying…"—to confirm you've understood correctly.
- **Stay calm and patient:** Keep your emotions in check, speak in a steady voice, and give the other person time to gather their thoughts.
- **Use positive language:** Replace criticism with constructive feedback. For example, say, "Please let me finish before you respond," rather than "Stop interrupting me!"
- **Aim for mutual understanding:** Seek to ensure both sides feel heard and respected, prioritizing connection over being right.

Active listening strengthens relationships, builds trust, and leads to more productive conversations—especially on difficult topics. By practicing these techniques, we can shift from conflict to meaningful dialogue.

Our goal is to reduce unplanned pregnancies to reduce stress on women and reduce abortions. We can do this together!

"Every good conversation starts with good listening."
~unknown

"Be a good listener. Encourage others to talk about themselves."
~Dale Carnegie

"Listening is an art that requires attention over talent, spirit over ego, others over self."
~Dean Jackson

Chapter 4

Empathy

Empathy (noun): the action of understanding, being aware of, being sensitive to, and vicariously experiencing the feelings, thoughts, and experience of another (Merriam Webster)

Mastering empathy can make you a more powerful, respected, and likable person. The word "empathy" comes from Latin and Greek roots: *em* (Latin) means "to see through," and *pathy* (Greek) means "the eye of the other." In other words, to empathize is to see through someone else's eyes.

Empathy is different from sympathy. **Sympathy** is feeling concern for someone experiencing pain or hardship. **Empathy** goes deeper—it means emotionally connecting with their experience. It doesn't require liking, loving, or even agreeing with the person. It simply means understanding their feelings and perspective.

Empathy is essential for healthy relationships and effective communication. It helps regulate emotions, strengthens connections, and even motivates us to help others. When we empathize, we step into another person's world, seeing and feeling from their perspective.

Ways to Build Empathy:
- **Practice active listening:** Avoid interrupting and focus on truly hearing others.
- **Seek to understand, not just to respond:** Even if you disagree, try to see their perspective.
- **Ask questions:** Learn about people's experiences, beliefs, and worldviews.
- **Put yourself in their shoes:** Imagine what they're feeling and why.
- **Connect on common ground:** Focus on similarities rather than differences.
- **Identify personal biases:** Recognize how they might shape your empathy.
- **Be open and vulnerable:** Share your own feelings to build mutual understanding.
- **Experience new things:** Stepping outside your comfort zone can give insight into different perspectives.

Empathy allows us to engage in difficult conversations with compassion and understanding. When discussing abortion—especially with those who hold opposing views—empathy is not just helpful, it's essential.

Our goal is to reduce unplanned pregnancies to reduce stress on women and reduce abortions. We can do this together!

"Empathy is seeing with the eyes of another, listening with the ears of another, and feeling with the heart of another."
~Alfred Adler

"Empathy works so well because it does not require a solution. It requires only understanding."
~John Medina

"Empathy is about finding echoes of another person in yourself."
~Mohsin Hamid

Chapter 5

Definitions are Important

The Importance of Defining Terms

Clear communication depends on well-defined terms. In everyday language, we assume certain words have a shared meaning based on context. Without this, understanding would be nearly impossible. However, words can carry different meanings for different people.

Take the word "dope." Traditionally, it means a foolish person (think Dopey from *Snow White*). To others, it refers to drugs like marijuana, originating from the idea that people who are high look foolish (think about any stoned movie character you've seen). Athletes might associate it with illegal performance-enhancing drugs. In casual slang, "dope" can mean something is excellent, while in parts of the Midwest, it's a topping for ice cream, such as chocolate syrup or fruit sauce.

Without precise definitions, discussions can become frustrating and confusing. Understanding a word's meaning does not mean accepting or agreeing with it—it simply means both parties are using the same definition. If two people define "dope" as "excellent," they can debate whether my singing is dope or not. Spoiler: it's not. But hey, I've accepted that I won't be a rock star—good thing I kept my day job!

Another example is the phrase "I slept with him." Literally, this should mean "resting in a state of sleep." In reality, it's a softer, more socially acceptable way of saying, "I had sex with him." People use euphemisms like this to make statements feel less harsh, judgmental, or stigmatizing.

This brings us to the heart of the discussion: honesty.

Honesty and Self-Reflection

In counseling, honesty—with ourselves and others—is key to self-awareness, growth, and positive change. Honesty is "adherence to the facts" and a refusal to deceive oneself or another person.

For example, if I'm overweight and out of shape and I'm not honest with myself about it, I'll never take steps to improve my health. I might even attempt a physically demanding activity I'm unprepared for, putting myself at risk. Facing reality, being honest, is the first step toward progress.

The same principle applies to abortion. Many in our culture minimize or overexaggerate the facts about abortion, using language to make it seem less or more harsh or controversial.

A common example is how each side might discuss safety and risk:
- A pro-choice person might say, "Abortion is completely safe and risk-free," emphasizing its routine nature and downplaying that, like any medical procedure, it carries risks.
- In contrast, a pro-life person might claim, "Abortion often damages a woman's reproductive system, making it hard

for her to have children later on." It's true legal abortions can possibly impair a woman's future fertility, especially with multiple abortions, however, overall it is statistically minimal.

Into my twenties, I identified as pro-choice, believing that a fetus was merely a cluster of cells. This perspective shifted after a female nurse friend shared videos and images with me, educating me about fetal development and abortion procedures. I learned that this topic and the emotions behind it are more complex than I'd originally thought. As a school counselor at the time skilled in active listening, I engaged with these materials earnestly, reflecting on my emotions and seeking to understand the scientific aspects. This process led to a profound change in my viewpoint.

Maybe your perspective will change, or maybe it won't. But my goal is simple: to educate. If this book leaves you more informed about abortion than you were before, then you've practiced active listening and empathy, and that's a win in itself.

Now, let's define key terms related to abortion. Whether this is new information or a review, I encourage you to engage with it openly, be honest with yourself, and reflect on how these facts make you feel—and why.

My goal is to educate, foster understanding, and find common ground—because at the end of the day, we are all part of the same human race. Please know that my purpose in writing this book is not to judge, criticize, or make anyone feel bad.

This is a deeply emotional and complex topic, and my hope is to reduce hostility and encourage a solution-focused mindset. If we can have honest, respectful conversations, we might discover we have more in common than we think.

Our goal is to reduce unplanned pregnancies to reduce stress on women and reduce abortions. We can do this together!

"The beginning of wisdom is a definition of terms."
~Socrates

"Definitions are the foundation of reason.
You cannot reason without them."
~Robert M. Pirsig

"Pedagogically (when teaching), we need definitions and borders.
They help us get our heads around what we're talking about."
~John D'Agata

Part 2

Let's Address This Difficult Matter with Honesty and Authenticity

Remember – deep breath, active listening, empathy …

Chapter 6

Definition of Abortion

First, let's define what the abortion law is in the United States of America.

History

Abortion became legal nationally in 1973, when Roe v. Wade came before the U.S. Supreme Court. In a landmark decision, 410 U.S. 113, the Court ruled that the Constitution of the United States generally protected a right to have an abortion.

The 1973 U.S. Supreme Court made the ruling, and American citizens did *not* vote for it, which was controversial at the time.

Current

In 2022, in the case of Dobbs v. Jackson Women's Health Organization, the U.S. Supreme Court made a landmark decision, 597 U.S. 215 (2022), ruling that the Constitution of the United States *does not* confer a right to abortion. The court's decision overruled both Roe v. Wade (1973) and Planned Parenthood v. Casey (1992), returning to individual states the power to regulate any aspect of abortion not protected by federal statutory law. (Dobbs vs. Jackson Women's Health Organization 2022)

Just like in 1973 for Roe v. Wade, the 2022 U.S. Supreme Court made the ruling, and it was *not* voted for by citizens of the United States, which was, again, controversial.

The Shifting Debate on Abortion in America

For the past five decades, abortion has been one of the most divisive issues in the United States. The Supreme Court's decision to overturn Roe v. Wade in 2022 shifted this debate from a national battle to a state-level issue, allowing each state to create its own abortion laws.

This shift makes sense in many ways. Some states lean strongly pro-choice, while others are overwhelmingly pro-life. Instead of a one-size-fits-all federal law, each state now has the ability to set policies that reflect the views of its residents. This approach aligns with the principles of America as a constitutional republic, giving voters more control over laws that directly impact them by voting for elected state representatives who align with their views and values.

As time has passed since this decision, the national political tension over abortion has eased somewhat. While some activists and politicians continue to push for federal abortion policies—either for or against—most of the debate now happens at the state level. This localized approach has, in many ways, reduced national division and allowed for more focused discussions within individual states.

Of course, not everyone is happy with this outcome. Pro-choice advocates living in largely pro-life states face political challenges in protecting abortion access. Meanwhile, pro-life supporters living in mostly pro-choice states face similar struggles in restricting it. However, these battles are now happening through state legislatures and local elections, rather than being dictated by a single Supreme Court ruling.

For those who value state-level democracy, this shift is seen as a win—giving citizens a greater voice in shaping their own laws. However, for those who believe abortion rights should be determined at the federal level, the debate continues. The reality is that the United States remains a free country, and individuals who strongly oppose their states' stances on abortion have the freedom to choose to relocate to states that better align with their values.

Okay, this discussion is getting real. Remember, deep breath, active listening, empathy. Deep breath, active listening, empathy. Regardless of how you feel about current legislation in America...

Our goal is to reduce unplanned pregnancies to reduce stress on women and reduce abortions. We can do this together!

Defining Abortion

Pro-choice and pro-life advocates often use very different definitions of abortion, shaping how they frame the debate.

- Pro-choice supporters define abortion in terms of women's rights and health care:
    - "Abortion is a right."
    - "Abortion is health care."
    - "Abortion is reproductive freedom."
    - "Abortion is a personal decision."

- Pro-life advocates define abortion in terms of the human fetus's rights and the ethics of ending a life:

- "Abortion is murder."
- "Abortion kills a person."
- "Abortion stops a human heart from beating."
- "Abortion denies unborn females a choice."

With such contrasting perspectives, it's no surprise that the conversation often turns into shouting matches rather than productive discussions. Each side focuses on a different set of rights—one on the woman's autonomy, the other on the fetus's life. To move beyond the conflict, both sides must first submit to a neutral, factual definition of abortion from a universally accepted and credible source.

A good starting point is the Merriam-Webster dictionary definition of abortion, as it may be used in medical, legal, and academic contexts.

Abortion (noun): the *termination* of a *pregnancy* after, accompanied by, resulting in, or closely *followed by the death of the embryo or fetus*: such as:

a. spontaneous expulsion of a human fetus during the first 12 weeks of gestation

b. induced expulsion of a human fetus

Terminate (transitive verb)

1: to bring to an end: close

2: to serve as an ending, limit, or boundary of

3: assassinate, kill

Pregnant (adjective): containing a developing embryo, fetus, or unborn offspring within the body (womb)

Offspring (noun): the product of the reproductive processes of a person, animal, or plant

person (noun): human, individual

Putting the definitions together we get:
A woman who contains a developing embryo, fetus, or unborn human within her womb (called pregnancy) chooses to have a procedure to end the development of the embryo, fetus, or unborn human (called terminate) followed by the death of the embryo, fetus, or unborn human within her body (called abortion).

What Does This Mean in Simple Terms?

More simply put, abortion is, **"ending the life of a developing human inside a mother's womb."** As clear as this is, there will still be some who will try to choose to use another definition, such as— "a personal choice regarding pregnancy and bodily autonomy." Respectfully, this is not the definition of abortion. While humans do have the freedom to make their own choices, every decision comes with outcomes, consequences, and impacts.

Regardless of one's stance, discussing abortion requires active listening, empathy, and an open mind to understand the complexity of the issue.

Deep breath, active listening, empathy.

Think about the classic sci-fi movie *The Terminator*. In the film, a cyborg assassin (Arnold Schwarzenegger) is sent from the future to hunt down a young woman named Sarah Connor because she is destined to give birth to a future leader named John Conner, who will save mankind. The mission? Eliminate Sarah—or her unborn child, John—before the future hero is ever born to save the world.

Now, imagine if the Terminator had succeeded. If Sarah Connor had been "terminated," or if her zygote/embryo/fetus/unborn child, John, had been "terminated," the future resistance would never exist and humanity would be doomed.

This might be a fictional scenario, but it reflects the real-world weight of decisions involving life and potential. The question at the heart of the abortion debate is: At what point does a developing human life have rights? Biologically, the zygote/embryo/fetus/yet-to-be born baby, John Conner in this case, remains a living, developing human regardless of his being wanted or not. The debate, therefore, is not about whether an embryo is alive, but whether it has rights. Did John Conner have rights before he was born?

True-Life Story - Cristiano Ronaldo

John Connor's story was fiction. Here's a true-life story. Soccer star Cristiano Ronaldo's mother, Maria Dolores dos Santos Aveiro, released an autobiography, *Mother Courage*, in which she told the story of how Cristiano Ronaldo almost didn't exist. She revealed that he was the result of an unplanned pregnancy, and she did everything she could to try to get an abortion. However, doctors disagreed with her decision, and despite her attempts, the abortion didn't happen.

After a doctor refused to abort the unborn baby, Aveiro said she tried a "home recipe." She went on to explain how she drank warm ale and "ran till she dropped," without achieving her aim. She later told *Daily Mail*, "I wanted to have an abortion but God did not want that to happen… Cristiano was an unwanted baby but he's given me so much joy." (Al-Samarrai 2015)

Portuguese footballer Cristiano Ronaldo is the most followed person in the world, with 651 million followers on Instagram at the time of this writing in 2025. He was indeed born and has ruled the soccer world for a long period. What if he had been terminated and was not alive to inspire so many people? Cristiano was obviously alive in his mother's womb from conception, but did Cristiano have rights before he was born?

Facing Reality with Honesty

The reality is simple: When a woman is happy about her pregnancy, she recognizes her unborn child as a living human being from the moment of conception or the moment she finds out she has conceived. She immediately takes steps to ensure her baby's health—seeking prenatal care, eating well, and preparing for birth.

She researches baby names. Her friends and family throw her a baby shower. She and her partner might host a gender-reveal party. She feels her baby kick, she talks or sings to her baby, and the father-to-be may do the same. Together, they prepare a nursery, read baby books, and anticipate the child's arrival with love and excitement.

The key point? If a pregnancy is wanted, there is no debate—the baby is acknowledged as a living human with rights from conception. No one questions it. Everyone celebrates it.

But if the pregnancy is unwanted, some still try to argue that the same developing human is not alive. Some argue that until a certain point in development, such as viability (the ability to survive outside the womb—which gets earlier and earlier with new technology continually being advanced), a developing embryo or fetus is not yet a "person" with legal rights and protections. Others may view an early embryo or fetus as a collection of cells with the potential for life, but not yet having the attributes that define a person or independent human being.

The truth is, whether planned or unplanned, the developing human zygote (fertilized egg), embryo, or fetus *is* a person, a living human inside the womb, a separate being from his or her mother. Denying this fact does not change the truth, this reality.

As we defined in simple terms earlier, an abortion *ends the life of a developing human inside the mother's womb*. If the fetus were not a living being, there would be nothing to abort. This is a fundamental truth that we must acknowledge if we aim to be honest, humane, and logical people.

If you're reading this book today, it means your mother carried you through pregnancy instead of aborting you. Whether as a human zygote from conception, an embryo, or a fetus, you were and are, a living human being from conception. A person. *Life does not come from non-life* (The Biogenesis Law). That's basic science, and simple logic follows: **If you are alive today, you have been a living human being/person since the moment you were conceived.**

I was a living human when conceived, my kids were living humans when conceived, you were a living human when conceived. Everyone I know was a living human when conceived … even though I can think of a few people who are a little odd and who may have been hatched, but that's a story for another time.

The Question at the Core: When Does Life Have Rights?

A central issue in the abortion debate is this: When does a developing human acquire rights? Scientifically, human life/development is a continuous process from conception:

- A *zygote* (fertilized egg) contains a complete set of human DNA separate from its mother's.
- An *embryo* (2-9 weeks) undergoes rapid growth and organ formation.
- A *fetus* (9 weeks onward) exhibits heartbeat, movement, and neurological development.

Cristiano Ronaldo and the rest of us were all once a living human zygote, embryo, fetus, baby, toddler, child, etc. from conception. There's no argument there. The disagreement lies in when legal and moral recognition begins. If the argument that we are living human beings from conception rings true, then doesn't it make sense to have legal and moral human rights from conception? I know my thought, I'll let you have yours.

A Solution Forward: Reducing Unplanned Pregnancies

Rather than focusing on differences and entrenching division, let us focus on a productive approach involving reducing the number of unplanned pregnancies through:

- Comprehensive sex education
- Increased access to contraception
- Support for women facing unplanned/unintended/unwanted pregnancies
- Eliminating actions that lead to unplanned pregnancies.

A balanced discussion on abortion requires intellectual honesty, scientific clarity, and a focus on solutions rather than conflict.

Our goal is to reduce unplanned pregnancies to reduce stress on women and reduce abortions. We can do this together.

"To deny people their human rights is to challenge their very humanity."
~Nelson Mandela

"I know nothing of man's rights, or woman's rights;
human rights are all that I recognize."
~Sarah Moore Grimke

"We hold these truths to be self-evident, that all men are created equal, that they are endowed by their Creator with certain unalienable Rights, that among these are Life, Liberty and the pursuit of Happiness."
~United States of America's Declaration of Independence

Chapter 7

Abortion Procedures

Understanding the Definition in Context

Now that we have established a shared definition of abortion, "ending the life of a developing human inside the mother's womb," from a neutral, widely recognized source (Merriam-Webster), this definition will serve as the foundation for the discussion moving forward.

To gain a fuller understanding of abortion, it is important to move beyond definitions and examine the medical procedures involved. What exactly happens during an abortion? What do these procedures look like at different stages of pregnancy?

Coming up, we will break down the different abortion methods, explaining what each one entails to provide a clear, factual picture of the process.

Understanding the Reality of Abortion Procedures

Abortion is a procedure that occurs almost one million times per year in the United States and 73 million times per year worldwide, according to the Guttmacher Institute and World Health Organization (WHO). (Worldometers 2025) Given the scale of these procedures, it's important to understand them fully. My hope is that after learning about these methods, we can work together to reduce unplanned pregnancies, thereby reducing stress on women and the number of abortions worldwide.

The Biological Basis of Human Life

To be fully informed, let's start with some basic biology. One fundamental scientific principle is that life does not originate from non-life—this is a core concept in biology. In previous sections, we defined the term "developing" as describing growth, differentiation, and transformation, all of which require the organism to be *alive.*

Let's take a moment to review human development:
- **Zygote (Week 1):** The moment a human male sperm fertilizes a woman's egg, a unique human life begins. At this instant, genetic traits and biological sex (XX for female, XY for male) and individualized DNA are determined.
- **Embryo (Weeks 2-9):** The fertilized egg undergoes rapid cell division and differentiation, forming the foundation for all organ systems.
- **Fetus (Week 9 to Birth):** Growth continues as organs develop and bodily systems mature.
- **Newborn:** Recently born.
- **Infant:** A child in the first period of life.
- **Child:** A young person especially between infancy and puberty.
- **Teenager:** Someone who is between 13 and 19 years old.
- **Adult:** A human being after an age (such as 18 or 21) specified by law. Physiologically, the human brain isn't considered fully developed until age 25+.

Each stage represents a continuation of the **same human life**, simply at different stages in its natural development.

Every person alive today once existed at these earlier stages. Before fertilization, the sperm and egg were separate cells, but once fertilization occurs at conception, a new, genetically distinct living human organism exists.

FUN FACT: Out of the millions of sperm released during fertilization, only *one* successfully reached and fertilized your mother's egg—and that one became YOU! If it had been a different sperm, you wouldn't be here. Think about it: **You literally won the very first race of your life!** Congratulations!

TRIVIA: The two youngest premature births on record occurred at 21 weeks gestation. Curtis Means and Richard Hutchinson were born one month apart in 2020 during the COVID-19 pandemic. Richard held the title of Guinness World Record-holder for the most premature baby in the world to survive until Curtis was born one month later and became the new Guinness World Record-holder. They both weighed under one pound. James Eldin Gill needs a mention here because he was the previous world-record holder, but he was born in 1987, when the technology wasn't anywhere near today. Incredible! (Oldest.org 2022)

Now that we've reviewed the biology, the next step is to examine the specific abortion procedures used at different stages of pregnancy. What actually happens during an abortion? What do these procedures involve? Let's take a closer look.

Understanding Abortion Procedures

Surprisingly, many people don't fully understand the most common abortion procedures. Discussions about these methods are often censured, and the reasons why could be debated at length—but that's beyond the scope of this book.

However, if we want an honest conversation about abortion, we must address what actually happens during these procedures. Without that knowledge, it's impossible to have an informed discussion.

Abortion procedures vary depending on how far along the pregnancy is. There are two main types:

1. **Chemical/Drug Abortion** (also called the Abortion Pill): This involves taking prescription drugs to end a pregnancy. It is approved by the Food & Drug Administration (FDA) for use for up to 10 weeks of pregnancy and works by blocking hormones needed for pregnancy to continue.

2. **Surgical Abortion:** A doctor performs a procedure in a clinic, medical office, or hospital to remove the embryo or fetus, ending the pregnancy. Most abortions are outpatient, meaning the patient does not stay overnight.

Both procedures are used in millions of cases worldwide each year. Understanding them is essential to any meaningful conversation about abortion.

Disclaimer

- **This book is for educational purposes only and is NOT medical advice.** The descriptions provided are basic overviews and do not cover all medical details, eligibility requirements, risks, symptoms, dangers, warnings, side effects, or potential complications. Consult a licensed medical professional for comprehensive medical information and guidance.

- **Abortion procedures vary by state.** The availability, legal status, and timing restrictions for these procedures differ depending on state and local laws. Check official state resources to understand what is permitted in your area.

Chemical/Drug/Medication Abortion

Chemical abortion is the most common abortion method. As of 2024, it accounted for approximately 60% of all abortions in the United States.

This procedure is often referred to as "medication abortion," but this term can be misleading. By definition, the word "medication" refers to substances "used to treat or manage illnesses." The primary drug used, mifepristone (also known by the names Mifeprex, Cytotec, RU-486, or simply the abortion pill), was first approved by the FDA on September 28, 2000. However, it was *not* developed to treat a disease or illness but strictly to induce pregnancy termination, to end the life of a developing human in a mother's womb.

In pharmacology, a drug is a chemical substance, typically of known structure, which, when administered to a living organism, produces a biological effect.

For clarity, this book will use the term "chemical abortion" to refer to this particular process.

What Is Chemical Abortion?

A chemical abortion terminates an early pregnancy with the use of prescription drugs, usually a two-step regimen:
1. **Mifepristone:** This drug blocks the effects of progesterone, a hormone necessary to sustain pregnancy.
2. **Misoprostol:** Taken 24–48 hours later, this drug induces uterine contractions, expelling the human embryo from the uterus.

In the United States, chemical abortion is typically available up to 10 weeks of pregnancy (measured from the first day of the last menstrual period).

To understand how mifepristone works, it's important to first understand progesterone, often called the "pregnancy hormone."

According to the Cleveland Clinic, "Progesterone plays a crucial role in maintaining pregnancy. It thickens the uterine lining to support a fertilized egg, prevents contractions that could lead to miscarriage, and helps regulate the immune system to tolerate the developing embryo" (2022).

During pregnancy, progesterone levels increase significantly each trimester, ensuring:

- A thick uterine lining, providing nutrients for the embryo

- Relaxation of uterine muscles, preventing premature contractions

- Breast tissue development, preparing for breastfeeding

Because progesterone is essential for sustaining a pregnancy, blocking it with mifepristone leads to the withholding of nutrients from the embryo, the breakdown of the uterine lining, the detachment and demise of the embryo, and, ultimately, the termination of the pregnancy.

Now that we understand what progesterone is, here are the usual two steps to a chemical abortion in more detail. A chemical abortion is a two-step process using drugs to end an early pregnancy.

Step 1: Administer Mifepristone

The first drug, mifepristone, blocks the effects of the hormone progesterone, which is essential for maintaining pregnancy. Without progesterone, the uterine lining breaks down, similar to what happens during a menstrual period. The placenta, which develops from the uterine lining, is responsible for providing oxygen and nutrients to the developing embryo or fetus. The placenta connects to the embryo via the umbilical cord and facilitates the exchange of nutrients/oxygen and waste products between the mother and the fetus. In short, mifepristone breaks the uterine lining down which prevents the placenta from developing, thus cutting off nutrients and oxygen to the developing embryo or fetus, stopping its growth.

Mifepristone alone successfully terminates about 75% of pregnancies, but, in many cases, the embryo or fetus is not expelled from the uterus. If the terminated embryo or fetus remains in the uterus, it can increase the risk of infection, sepsis, and other complications.

Step 2: Administer Misoprostol

To complete the process, a second drug—misoprostol—is taken 24 to 48 hours later. Misoprostol causes:

- The uterus to contract and the cervix to soften, helping expel the embryo or fetus
- Cramping and bleeding, similar to a heavy period or miscarriage
- The embryo or fetus to pass, typically while the woman is at home, meaning that any embryo waste is flushed down the toilet, including the blood and placental tissue

Most women experience strong cramping, nausea, and bleeding as the embryo/fetus is expelled. In some cases, if the embryo/fetus is not fully expelled, a follow-up medical procedure (such as a dilation and curettage, or D&C) may be needed to prevent infection.

By taking the two drugs together, what a woman is doing is essentially inducing a miscarriage.

A woman can take both pills either by mouth or by inserting them into her vagina. These pills may cause heavy vaginal bleeding, strong cramps, nausea and vomiting, fever and chills, tiredness or weakness, headache, diarrhea, or dizziness.

A woman can use nonprescription pain relievers to ease discomfort, or her doctor can give her a prescription for pain medication. A chemical abortion is usually complete about two to six hours after a woman takes the second pill, though it can sometimes take longer. After a day or two, her bleeding should lessen. She may have light bleeding for several weeks.

A woman needs to follow up with her health care provider to make sure the abortion was completed. A urine test taken at home cannot show right away whether the abortion was successful because pregnancy hormones remain high for up to a month. But a blood test or an ultrasound can confirm it about a week after a woman takes the drugs. If the baby is still alive, she may need more medication or a surgical abortion.

Surgical Abortions

Vacuum Aspiration (Suction Abortion)

Vacuum aspiration, also known as suction abortion, is the most commonly performed in-clinic abortion worldwide. It is typically used up to 15 weeks of pregnancy; by now the fetus is working on breathing, sucking, and swallowing motions for when it's outside the womb; it's kicking, curling toes, and moving its arms and legs, and its heartbeat can be heard.

Before the procedure, the cervix (the lower part of the uterus) is softened and dilated to allow for the safe passage of medical instruments. This may be done using:

- **Drugs** such as mifepristone and misoprostol, which soften the cervix and may cause cramping and bleeding, and
- **Dilapan rods**, which are small, absorbent rods that expand over time to gently open the cervix

Once the cervix is prepared, a thin tube is inserted into the uterus, and suction is used to extract the still-alive fetus and placenta piece by piece.

Pain relief for the woman may be offered in the form of local anesthesia, oral pain medication, or light sedation.

Dilation and Evacuation (D&E)

Dilation and evacuation (D&E) is performed after 15 weeks of pregnancy. This is during the second and third trimester, when the fetus's taste buds are forming and connecting to its brain, becoming fully developed by week 20; it can move all joints and limbs freely and is constantly active. It now has distinct facial features—eyelids, eyebrows, eyelashes, nails, and hair—and is practicing behaviors like thumb-sucking, yawning, and stretching.

This procedure also requires cervical dilation, which is done over several hours or up to a day before the procedure. The abortion provider uses a combination of suction and surgical instruments (forceps) to dismember and extract the still-alive fetus in sections.

The procedure usually takes 10 to 20 minutes, and most patients go home the same day. Conscious sedation or general anesthesia may be used.

Intact Dilation and Extraction (Intact D&E, D&X, or IDX)

This procedure is used in the second and third trimester and is sometimes referred to as a "partial-birth abortion" when performed without first inducing fetal demise.

In the U.S., performing this method on a living fetus is banned under the Partial-Birth Abortion Ban Act of 2003, unless certain medical exceptions apply. However, the procedure may still be performed in some countries.

The process involves:
1. Turning the living fetus toward a breech (feet-first) position
2. Delivering the body while keeping the head inside the uterus
3. Using surgical instruments to puncture the skull and suction out the brain, causing the skull to collapse for removal

While the surgery itself takes about 30 minutes, the overall procedure, including cervical preparation, takes 2–3 days.

Processing what we just read:

I don't know if reading about these procedures made you pause for a moment, feel unsettled, or even tugged at your heartstrings. If it did, that's understandable. Abortion is a complex and deeply personal issue, and discussing it openly—without avoiding the realities—can be challenging.

From one human to another, I believe we can be better humans than this and work together to **reduce unplanned pregnancies**, so that these procedures become less frequent and we can be more humane humans. No matter where you stand on this issue, we can likely agree that preventing unplanned pregnancies through education, resources, and support is a goal worth pursuing.

For those who feel sympathy or empathy for the unborn child—who never had a voice in the decision—it's okay to sit with that emotion. At the same time, it's also important to recognize the struggles and decisions that lead women to seek abortion in the first place.

If we approach this discussion with understanding rather than judgment, we might find more common ground than we realize.

To effectively reduce unplanned pregnancies, it is imperative to prioritize research and development of safer, more effective, and longer-lasting contraceptive methods. This includes expanding options for both women and men. Recent advancements, such as the development of a hormone-free male birth control pill that reversibly stops sperm production and is currently undergoing human trials, demonstrate promising progress in this area (Feltman et al. 2025).

Additionally, ongoing research focuses on innovative contraceptive technologies, such as long-acting vaginal rings and low-dose copper intrauterine devices (IUDs), aiming to provide more choices that align with individuals' diverse needs and preferences.

Investing in these advancements is crucial to addressing the unmet need for family planning and empowering individuals with effective tools to prevent unintended pregnancies.

Abortion Percentages

According to the World Population Review (2025):

> When considering the rationale for people who choose to have an abortion, the number of abortions related to incest and rape is extremely low. Instead, most women choose to have an abortion because having a baby at that point in time would drastically change their lives. About 75% of women said a baby would negatively impact their lives, while 74% of women said they would not be able to afford a child, which has led to a decision to have an abortion. Almost half of the women asked, forty-eight percent, said they chose to have an abortion because they did not want to be a single mother, while 38% of women said they were already finished having children.

> At the opposite end of the spectrum, only 1% of all women had an abortion because it was a result of rape, and 0.5% of women had an abortion because it was the result of an incestuous relationship. However, many of these statistics may be skewed because of the overwhelming number of rapes that are not reported. When it comes to rape or incest, shame, fear of judgment, and lack of control may all play a part in why rapes go unreported.

Our goal is to reduce unplanned pregnancies to reduce stress on women and reduce abortions. We can do this together!

Chapter 8

Pro-Choice:
Every Person's Story Matters

Many women struggle deeply with the decision to have abortions. Over years of counseling, I've found that most women who choose abortion do so because they feel trapped in crises.

Crisis (noun):

1a: the turning point for better or worse in an acute disease or fever

1b: a paroxysmal attack of pain, distress, or disordered function

1c: an emotionally significant event or radical change of status in a person's life

2:   the decisive moment

3a: an unstable or crucial time or state of affairs in which a decisive change is impending especially: one with the distinct possibility of a highly undesirable outcome

3b: a situation that has reached a critical phase

A crisis is a turning point, a moment of distress, or an unstable situation in which a big decision must be made. For many women, an unexpected pregnancy feels like a crisis because they fear undesirable outcomes—financial struggles, lack of support, or drastic life changes.

Some women see abortion as just another form of birth control, but this book is not about them. It's for the average woman I've seen in counseling who felt lost, pressured, or scared when facing unplanned pregnancies. Whether she made the decision alone or with others or was coerced, she felt overwhelmed in that moment.

Instead of judging, we should listen carefully and show empathy. Understanding a woman's feelings and struggles is key to helping her prevent unplanned pregnancy, navigating her choices in the case of an unplanned pregnancy, and/or easing the pain that may come after an abortion.

Here are four typical stories I've come across over the years. Names have been changed.

Mary (Continued from Chapter 1)
"I was 18 at the end of high school when I discovered I was pregnant. I grew up with a hardworking single mom of three, and as the oldest, I felt immense pressure. The man involved had just become my ex—a 21-year-old college junior with the maturity of a 15-year-old, still living off his parents and known for his womanizing and controlling behavior.

I kept the pregnancy a secret to shield my already overburdened mom and to avoid any lasting connection with him. Although I had always dreamed of having children and a family, I wasn't ready—emotionally, mentally, or financially—to raise a child on my own. Abortion seemed like my only option. The clinic treated the procedure as routine, so I didn't think of it as anything too major. When I returned home, I simply told my mom I had the flu.

It wasn't until 10 years later, after having my first child, that I fully grasped the gravity of my decision. While I strive to live without regrets, I mourned what I had lost and kept my experience secret for 20 years. Eventually, sharing my story brought a sense of relief, especially when met with empathy by others with similar experiences."

Kristin

"I was 24, graduated from college, and starting my career. I met a guy and we had been dating off and on for a few months, but he was starting his career as well, so neither of us was looking for anything serious. We were just enjoying each other's company and having fun when our schedules allowed. Then one month I missed my period, took a pregnancy test, and it was positive.

I waited a few days to process and confirm with my doctor. When confirmed, I called the guy I was dating and we met for dinner. I shared with him, curious what his response would be. It wasn't positive. I admit I had mixed emotions, but I didn't have any support from him or my family and I didn't feel I could do it on my own, so I felt that left only one option. The abortion wasn't a pleasant experience. I did it, I live with it. I'm now happily married with three beautiful children."

Ashley

"At the time, I was married for 10 years and we had two wonderful children ages 6 and 4. The 4-year-old was a treasure but had special needs. We didn't make a lot of money, so when I found out I was pregnant the thought of the added financial burden, having a newborn in diapers, needing daycare, etc. was too much for us to handle at that time.

My husband and I talked about it. We struggled with the decision, but we were barely making ends meet and people at his work were getting laid off. We decided an abortion was the way to go. He took me to the clinic and was very caring. We cried that night and then focused on our two children who are now teens. Our child with special needs is thriving, but still takes a lot of time, energy, and finances. We did what we thought we had to do, no looking back."

Jane

"During my freshman year of college, I joined a sorority. In the spring, I went with some sorority sisters to a frat party with a bunch of frat guys and athletes where alcohol and drugs were everywhere. As the night went on, I became intoxicated, lost track of my sorority sisters, and ended up alone in a bedroom with a guy I liked. He was trying to make out with me, but I told him no, that I felt sick. The room was spinning and I passed out—or was drugged.

When I woke up, I was naked, and a different guy who I didn't know was getting out of the bed with other guys in the room looking like they were waiting their turn. The realization of what had happened hit me like a wave of nausea, and I vomited on the floor. Ashamed and in shock, I stumbled around dizzily, getting dressed, and left while hearing crude remarks spewed at me.

Overwhelmed with guilt and fear, I took the morning-after pill, but it wasn't enough—after some time I found out I was pregnant. I thought my life was over. After a difficult decision, I chose what I knew in my heart was right for me; I had an abortion. I reported the assault/s and should have gone to the police right away, but I had waited several weeks and nothing came of it. He said, she said. Their word against mine, and they lied for each other. I had heard stories of this happening, but I never imagined it would happen to me.

I left school after that semester. Back home with counseling and the support of my family and friends, it was a long, difficult road, but I went through much healing and moved forward with my life."

Note: While publishing this book, I watched the film *Promising Young Woman* with a close friend who is an ER nurse and her teenage daughter. The movie, starring Carey Mulligan, portrays a woman seeking justice for her best friend who was sexually assaulted in college. As I watched, I was struck by the uncanny similarities between the film's plot and the above story of "Jane's" real-life experience, including some nearly identical lines. Although I'm certain Jane's story predates the film, the parallels were so strong that I worried readers might think her account was copied from the movie. My friend reassured me, noting that such stories from her experience are, unfortunately, all too common and to keep the story in this book. I mention this 1) to reinforce from an ER nurse's perspective the seriousness and commonality of this story, and 2) to encourage you to watch *Promising Young Woman* if you haven't already (viewer discretion is advised)—it offers a powerful depiction of sexual assault and the complex challenges survivors face in seeking justice.

Recognizing the Crisis

No matter what our personal opinions are, we must acknowledge that many women feel trapped and alone when facing unplanned pregnancies. In those moments, they believe they have no options. Empathy is key.

Research shows that one in four women in the U.S. will have an abortion by age 45. (Jones & Jerman 2017) That means if there are eight women in your social circle, at least two will have had abortions by their 40s.

Every woman who has had an abortion has her own story, reasons, and emotions. Some readers may even feel a mix of emotions right now. The stories shared earlier are common unplanned/ unintended pregnancy experiences, but there are also cases involving incest, pedophilia, prostitution, etc.—topics we will explore later.

Abortion Statistics

According to a Pew Research Center (Diamant et al. 2024) article, here are some abortion statistics:

> In the District of Columbia and the 46 states that reported age data to the CDC in 2021, the majority of women who had abortions (57%) were in their 20s, while about three in 10 (31%) were in their 30s. Teens ages 13 to 19 accounted for 8% of those who had abortions, while women ages 40 to 44 accounted for about 4%.

> The vast majority of women who had abortions in 2021 were unmarried (87%), while married women accounted for 13%, according to the CDC, which had data on this from 37 states.

> In the District of Columbia, New York City (but not the rest of New York), and the 31 states that reported racial and ethnic data on abortion to the CDC, 42% of all women who had abortions in 2021 were non-Hispanic Black, while 30% were non-Hispanic White, 22% were Hispanic, and 6% were of other races.

> For 57% of U.S. women who had induced abortions in 2021, it was the first time they had ever had one, according to the CDC. For nearly a quarter (24%), it was their second abortion. For 11% of women who had an abortion that year, it was their third, and for 8% it was their fourth or more.

Our goal is to reduce unplanned pregnancies to reduce stress on women and reduce abortions. We can do this together!

Chapter 9

Pro-Life: Every Person's Story Matters

True stories. Real names.

Josiah (Continued from Chapter 1)

In 1995, a woman in South Korea became pregnant while living with her partner. They already had a daughter and were struggling financially, so she decided to have an abortion at two months. The procedure—a curettage abortion—was meant to remove the baby in pieces. However, at five months, she realized the abortion had failed, and the baby was still growing.

At that point, the family chose adoption. On October 7, 1995, the baby— me—was born. I was healthy except for a deformed arm. I lived in a foster home until I was 13 months old, when I was adopted by a loving family in Norman, Oklahoma.

I had an active childhood—playing sports, joining Boy Scouts, and doing most things like any other kid. I was raised in a Christian home where abortion was clearly seen as wrong. So at 12 years old, when my parents told me that my birth mother had originally tried to abort me, I was shocked and heartbroken. I had always wanted to meet my birth parents and had respected their decision to place me for adoption. But learning the truth left me angry and even depressed—I struggled with the thought that my own birth parents hadn't wanted me.

With time, I chose forgiveness. Instead of dwelling on the past, I grew more grateful for my adoptive parents, who truly wanted me. Most of all, I thanked God—I believe He saved me for a purpose. Today, I use my story to speak out against abortion and help save lives. Being a survivor gives me a unique perspective, and people listen. In the end, I give all glory to God and trust that my life has a purpose in His plan. (The Life Institute 2022)

Nik

At 23, Nik Hoot has overcome more challenges than most do in a lifetime. In 1996 in Russia, his biological mother underwent a late-term abortion meant to end his life at 24 weeks—but Nik survived. Born prematurely without legs and some fingers, he was later adopted by a family in Indiana.

Although his adoptive mother, Apryl Hoot, initially felt unprepared to care for a child with prosthetic limbs, Nik quickly defied her fears. By age two, he discarded his walker and was running around the house. Apryl once hesitated to let him play sports, worried about potential teasing, but Nik not only participated, he excelled, playing baseball and wrestling, even reaching the state championships in high school.

Nik compares wrestling to life: "There's so much you don't want to do—hard work, conditioning. But that's just life. You're going to hit a lot of barriers, but you have to get over them."

Today, Nik works in landscaping and shares his inspiring story, reminding everyone that every life matters. "Anybody can become anything," he says. "Getting rid of a kid like that isn't right. I see myself as a miracle." (Bilger 2019)

Melissa

At 14, Melissa Ohden learned a shocking truth—her mother had tried to abort her. In 1977, Melissa's 19-year-old mother underwent an abortion at an Iowa hospital. Born at eight months and weighing less than three pounds, Melissa was left among medical waste. A nurse heard her weak cries and saved her life.

Doctors believed she might be blind or have a fatal heart defect, but she grew up completely healthy, raised by her adoptive family. She only discovered her past when her adoptive sister blurted it out during an argument. Struggling with the news, Melissa battled an eating disorder and alcohol abuse before deciding, at 19, to search for her birth mother.

It took over a decade, but when they finally reconnected, Melissa was shocked to learn that her mother never knew she had survived. Her grandmother, a nurse, had forced the abortion and kept Melissa's survival a secret.

Despite this painful past, Melissa doesn't hold anger. Instead, she feels grateful for both her adoptive and birth families. Now living in Kansas City near her birth mother and half-sister, she cherishes their relationship and the joy they share today. Melissa went on to become the founder of the Abortion Survivors Network. (Eley & Adnitt 2019)

Ashley

Ashley Lawton always knew she was adopted, but in high school, she was shocked to learn her birth mother was a rape survivor. "I remember driving with my mom when a song sparked a conversation," she recalls. "I said, 'I can't imagine being raped, becoming pregnant, and carrying that child.' My mom replied, 'Ashley, honey, your birth mother was raped.'"

In that moment, time seemed to stand still, and she could only hear, "You're a product of evil. You were never meant to be." Those words haunted her for years, even as her faith sustained her.

Over time, as she sought God, Ashley realized she was deeply loved and that every life holds value—planned or not. Now married and a mother of two, she has become a passionate advocate for life. She serves on the board of Personhood Carolina and supports Save The 1, a nonprofit helping those conceived in traumatic circumstances.

Ashley encourages Christians to support women facing crisis pregnancies with compassion. "Tell them it's not their fault, that God loves them, and they are stronger than they realize," she advises. She also warns that abortion can add further trauma, urging women to consider adoption. "I was conceived in rape—an act of violence—but I was innocent. I thank God that my birth mother valued life enough to give me a chance." (Deaton 2022).

Our goal is to reduce unplanned pregnancies to reduce stress on women and reduce abortions. We can do this together!

Chapter 10

Danger to Mother
and Birth Defect Abortions

According to the Lozier Institute (Gaitan et al. 2024), the reasons for seeking abortion are as follows: 95.9% elective and unspecified reasons; 2.2% other physical health concerns; 1.2% abnormality in the unborn baby; 0.4% rape and incest; and 0.3% risk to the woman's life or a major bodily function.

0.3% Risk to the Woman's Life or a Major Bodily Function

Here are six medical conditions in which abortion can be a life-saving choice, summarized from a 2024 *Everyday Health* article by Rachael Robertson:

1. Pulmonary Hypertension

   Pulmonary hypertension causes dangerously high blood pressure in the vessels between heart and lungs, forcing the heart to over-work. Pregnancy further strains the heart, doubling its workload. Without ending the pregnancy, there's up to a 50% chance of heart failure and death. In such cases, abortion can protect the mother's life.

2. Ectopic Pregnancy

An ectopic pregnancy happens when a fertilized egg implants outside the uterus—most often in a fallopian tube. Since the embryo cannot survive and the growing tissue can cause the tube to burst, this condition leads to life-threatening internal bleeding. Treating an ectopic pregnancy means ending it immediately to save the mother.

3. Severe Preeclampsia

Around mid-pregnancy, some develop severe preeclampsia—dangerously high blood pressure that can damage the brain, liver, kidneys, and other organs. If it arises before 24 weeks, delivering the fetus counts as abortion because the baby is unlikely to survive outside the womb. Even after 24 weeks, immediate delivery may be needed to prevent seizures, strokes, or organ failure. Once the pregnancy ends, preeclampsia resolves.

4. Advanced Kidney Disease

Pregnancy increases stress on the kidneys. In people with severe kidney disease, this extra burden can push them into kidney failure or trigger serious complications. When the health risks to both parent and fetus become too great, health care providers may advise ending the pregnancy.

5. Cancer

Treating cancer often involves radiation or certain drugs that can harm a developing fetus. If delaying treatment to carry a pregnancy jeopardizes the parent's health or life, abortion may be the safest option.

6. Lethal Fetal Anomalies

Some diagnoses—like anencephaly, where the baby's brain and skull do not fully form—mean the fetus cannot survive after birth. Continuing such pregnancies puts the parent through unnecessary physical and emotional trauma. Abortion in these cases is safer than full-term delivery and spares the mother additional risk.

Balancing Risks and Choices

In all these scenarios, the decision to have an abortion arises from weighing serious medical dangers against the desire to remain pregnant. Specialists in high-risk pregnancies guide patients through this process, helping them choose the option that best protects their health and well-being. In states where abortion access is restricted, parents may face added fear of legal consequences, complicating what is already a deeply personal and urgent medical choice.

Ultimately, when pregnancy poses a significant threat to life or health—whether from the parent's condition or a nonviable fetus—abortion can be an essential, even life-saving, medical intervention.

1.2% Abnormality in the Unborn Baby (Terminating for Medical Reasons, or TFMR)

Summarized from "Baby Loss Support" by Tommy's, The Pregnancy and Baby Charity website (2023):

All pregnant people are routinely offered screening tests to identify potential health issues in themselves or their babies. If a screening suggests an elevated risk of a serious condition—or if there's a known family history—diagnostic tests are offered to confirm whether the condition is present. These tests often take place at specialized fetal medicine units. Depending on the diagnosis, some conditions can be treated before or after birth, but others—known as fetal anomalies or birth defects—may lead to chronic illness, disability, stillbirth, or neonatal death. In rare cases, continuing a pregnancy also poses significant health risks to the mother.

When a diagnosis indicates severe harm to the baby or a dangerous complication for the parent, health care providers will discuss the option of ending the pregnancy. This choice remains with the individual, though if the mother's life is at risk, clinicians may strongly recommend termination.

If a health care professional deems the condition sufficiently serious to warrant discussion of termination, the person can request a second opinion —especially before 24 weeks' gestation, when the legal criteria for abortion become stricter.

Throughout this process, families are encouraged to gather as much information as possible, consulting various specialists and support organizations. Emotions can range from devastation over the loss of the healthy child they expected to guilt over considering termination; there is no right way to feel. Ultimately, parents must weigh medical risks against their desire to continue the pregnancy, supported by their health care team's guidance.

"When we went to our 20-week scan and found out our baby had not developed how he should have and that he would not survive after birth, we knew TFMR was the right thing to do for him, to protect him from any pain, regardless of how heartbreaking it was for us." – Katherine

On the flip side, I met Angela Bakker and she told the amazing story of her and her daughter, Naomi, beating the odds. In 2015, she and her unborn baby were both likely to die. "'Not viable with life,' they told us. 'If by some miracle she lives, she most likely won't walk,' they told us. 'Challenge accepted,' thought Naomi. We are so thankful for answered prayers and our living, walking, talking, laughing little medical anomaly (aka miracle),' the Bakkers explained." (Flanders 2023) Though there were some health issues along the way, today Naomi is a healthy young girl and a blessing to many.

As a school psychologist, counselor, and life coach, I constantly seek sources of motivation to keep my own emotional reserves full—and to inspire the people I work with. Tim Tebow—former NFL player and Heisman trophy winner, and, Nick Vujicic, widely regarded as one of the world's leading motivational speakers, never fail to uplift me. They both have birth stories that demonstrate how they're lucky to be here, and the world is a better place with them in it.

Tim Tebow's Birth Story

Tim Tebow's birth nearly ended before it began. While preaching in the Philippines in 1986, his father wept over global abortion rates and felt called to have another child. Though his mother was initially reluctant, she too came to believe the calling and soon became pregnant. Due to early scans showing complications and the belief that Tim was not a viable baby, Doctors advised her to abort, warning that both mother and child would die.

Refusing to give in, his parents trusted their faith. When Tim was born, only a tiny piece of placenta had attached, leaving him severely malnourished. The delivering physician called it "the greatest miracle I have ever seen," since no medical explanation could account for his survival.

Tim grew to be the largest of his four siblings, won the Heisman Trophy, played in the NFL, and has since dedicated his life to charity through his foundation, which hosts Night to Shine events for people with special needs. (Gordoni 2025)

The Tim Tebow Foundation (TTF) strives to fight for the Most Vulnerable People in the world—the MVPs—through its work with four main focuses: antihuman trafficking and child exploitation, orphan care + prevention, profound medical needs, and special needs ministry.

The Nick Vujicic Story

Nick was born in 1982 in Australia with tetra-amelia syndrome, a condition in which all four limbs are missing. His parents and doctors were shocked, having no inkling of his condition before his birth. Nick shares that the doctors said if they had known of the birth defect, they would have recommended an abortion.

It's been noted that Nick's mother initially refused to hold him, overwhelmed by grief and uncertainty. Nick later endured severe bullying at school and once nearly took his own life. Yet his parents became his greatest supporters, teaching him to focus on life's possibilities.

Today, Nick's message of hope reaches millions through talks, books, and his documentary, *No Limbs, No Limits – The Nick Vujicic Story*. (Nickvujicic.com 2025)

His story reminds me of the remarkable students with disabilities I support every day as a school psychologist—those with learning differences, autism, intellectual disabilities, physical challenges, health impairments, deafness or blindness, and many more. They may not speak on global stages, but each one shows extraordinary courage and inspires everyone around them, including me.

In a world that often values "normal," Nick Vujicic—and people like him—demonstrate that our true strength comes from resilience, faith, and the support of those who believe in us. Their stories encourage us all to embrace life's challenges and discover our own potential.

Our goal is to reduce unplanned pregnancies to reduce stress on women and reduce abortions. We can do this together!

"Sometimes I pretend to be normal, but it gets boring.
So I go back to being me."
~unknown~

"Who wants to be normal when you can be unique?"
~Helena Bonham Carter

"If you are always trying to be normal,
you'll never know how amazing you can be."
~Maya Angelou

"There is no normal life, there's just life. You live it."
~Val Kilmer

Chapter 11

Healing

As a mental health professional, I can't discuss this emotional and controversial topic without addressing its impact. Some women see abortion as a form of birth control and feel no distress. This chapter isn't for them.

This chapter is for those who have struggled emotionally after abortions. There's a saying: "Abortion has two victims." While not true for everyone, I've seen it affect many—teens, adults, sex workers, survivors of trafficking, married and single women, rich and poor, and those violated by rape and incest or reconciling possible birth defects. Pain after abortion isn't limited to one type of person—it can happen to anyone. Countless women suffer and have suffered in silence, many for decades.

Mental Health Concerns After Abortion and the Healing Process

Abortion is a complex and emotional decision that can have lasting mental health effects on both women and men. While some feel relief, others experience sadness, guilt, regret, anxiety, or depression. The emotional response varies based on personal beliefs, support systems, and circumstances surrounding the abortion. Studies show that some individuals struggle with long-term psychological distress, often referred to as post-abortion stress syndrome (PASS), though it is not officially recognized as a medical condition. The healing process involves emotional support, counseling, and self-care strategies to cope with the psychological impact of abortion.

Many women report mixed emotions after abortion. Initially, some feel relief, especially if the pregnancy was unplanned or occurred under difficult circumstances. However, over time, feelings of guilt, shame, and sadness may emerge, especially if the abortion conflicts with personal values or cultural and religious beliefs. A study published in the *British Journal of Psychiatry* found that women who had abortions were 81% more likely to experience mental health issues compared to those who had not. Depression, anxiety, substance abuse, and even suicidal thoughts are more common among those who struggle with their abortion decisions. (Coleman 2011)

Men can also be affected by abortion, especially if they had no say in the decision or if they regret encouraging it. Some men experience sadness, guilt, anger, or a sense of helplessness. Studies suggest that men who lose children to abortion may suffer from depression and relationship difficulties as they struggle with feelings of loss that society often overlooks. Many men do not seek help because they feel they are not allowed to grieve or express emotions about the abortion.

The healing process after an abortion varies, but counseling and emotional support play crucial roles. Postabortion counseling helps individuals process their emotions, work through grief, and find healthy coping mechanisms. Support groups provide safe spaces for women and men to share their experiences and connect with others who understand their pain. Faith-based counseling services are also available for those who seek spiritual healing. Studies show that individuals who receive post-abortion counseling are less likely to suffer from long-term mental health issues and have an easier time moving forward.

We mental health professionals have a saying, "If you don't speak it, you'll leak it." Meaning, if you don't talk with someone about it, like with God alone in your room, a therapist, or a trusted friend or family member, then usually the pain will manifest as anxiety, depression, mood swings, or even at-risk behaviors like drug and alcohol use and abuse, promiscuity, violence, suicidal thoughts/attempts, etc.

Self-care and emotional healing are essential after an abortion. Engaging in healthy activities like exercise, journaling, and mindfulness can help manage stress and emotional pain. It's important to acknowledge feelings rather than suppress them as unresolved grief can lead to ongoing emotional struggles.

While abortion affects people differently, it's essential to recognize that emotional healing takes time. Providing compassionate support, counseling, and resources for both women and men can help individuals process their experiences and find a path toward healing. Society must acknowledge the mental health impact of abortion and ensure that those struggling have access to the care they need to move forward.

Our goal is to reduce unplanned pregnancies to reduce stress on women and reduce abortions. We can do this together!

"Healing doesn't mean the damage never existed.
It means the damage no longer controls our lives."
~unknown

"You heal by releasing, not by suppressing."
~unknown

"Our brains are wired for connection, but trauma rewires them for protection. That's why healthy relationships are difficult for wounded people."
~Ryan North

"As soon as healing takes place, go out and heal somebody else."
~Maya Angelou

"Jesus said to her, 'Daughter, your faith has healed you.
Go in peace and be freed from your suffering.'"
Mark 5:34

"Forgiveness (for yourself and others) does not change the past, but it does change the future."
~Paul Lewis Boese

"Forgive others (and yourself) not because they deserve it, but because you deserve peace."
~Jonathan Lockwood Hule

"All healing starts with beginning to accept yourself and love yourself; even your flaws."
~Bryant McGill

RESOURCES

Note: Though I am familiar with some of these resources, I have not read and vetted all these books and websites. They were either recommended to me by sources I know personally or discovered as I conducted an internet search. Please do your own research to find what may be a good fit for you.

Most cities have some sort of crisis pregnancy center that may have in-person counseling and groups, and/or they may make recommendations for local therapists or books and websites that they have found fruitful in helping those who seek assistance postabortion.

Books:

• *The Healing Choice: Your Guide to Emotional Recovery After an Abortion* by Candace De puy and Dana Dovitch

• *You're Not Alone: Healing Through God's Grace After Abortion* by Jennifer O'Neill

• *A Solitary Sorrow: Finding Healing & Wholeness after Abortion* by Teri Reisser, with Paul Reisser

• *Forbidden Grief: The Unspoken Pain of Abortion* by Theresa Burke, with David C. Reardon

• *Moving Forward After Abortion: Finding Comfort in God (Ask the Christian Counselor)* by Camille Cates

• *Peace After Abortion* by Ava Torre-Bueno

Websites:

Support After Abortion
https://supportafterabortion.com

Human Life International
https://www.hli.org/resources/post-abortion-support-groups

Postpartum Support International
https://www.postpartum.net/group/post-abortion-support

Reproductive Health Access Project
https://www.reproductiveaccess.org/resource/counselingresources

Focus on the Family: Post-Abortive Recovery Resources
https://www.focusonthefamily.com/get-help/post-abortive-recovery-resources

Lumina: Hope and Healing After Abortion
https://postabortionhelp.org

Elliot Institute
https://afterabortion.org

Part 3

How to Reduce Unplanned Pregnancies

Chapter 12

Sexual Abstinence

Abstinence (noun):
1: the practice of abstaining from something: the practice of not doing or having something that is wanted or enjoyable
2a: habitual abstaining from intoxicating beverages
2b: abstention from sexual intercourse

Abstinence means choosing to avoid certain behaviors, like drinking alcohol, smoking, or engaging in sexual activity. "Sexual abstinence" specifically refers to refraining from sex. For some, this means waiting until marriage to have sex; for others, it may involve avoiding vaginal sex, or even any form of sexual contact like kissing or petting.

The most effective way to avoid unplanned pregnancies is through abstinence—in other words, simply not having sex. It's free, simple (though not always easy), and 100% effective.

Now, I know some of you might be thinking, "Dude, that's boring!" But hear me out—abstinence can offer benefits that might surprise you. While sex in the right context can be enjoyable, there are also many positives to choosing abstinence.

Benefits of Sexual Abstinence:

- **It prevents pregnancy:** The best way to avoid an *unplanned pregnancy* is not to have sex.

- **It prevents sexually transmitted infections *(STIs)*:** Abstinence eliminates the risk of diseases like chlamydia, gonorrhea, HIV, and more. The CDC reported in 2023 that one in five Americans has an STI, with young adults between ages 20 and 34 having the highest rates. In your social circle of 10 people, two of you have STIs.

- **It gives you time:** Abstinence can help you wait until you feel ready for a sexual relationship and until you find the right partner.

- **No birth control is needed:** If you don't have access to birth control—or don't want to use it—abstinence is a reliable option.

- **It supports emotional connections:** It helps you build meaningful relationships that are not based solely on sex, allowing for deeper emotional intimacy and trust.

- **It improves mental health:** By reducing anxiety related to sex, abstinence can boost your overall well-being. It can also help lower stress and avoid performance anxiety.

- **It reduces the risk of infections:** Abstaining can help reduce urinary tract infections and as mentioned before lowers the chance of developing an STI.

- **It promotes personal growth:** It allows you to focus on school, career goals, hobbies, and self-improvement, free from the distractions or pressures of sexual relationships.

- **It helps with emotional stability:** During tough times like a breakup or the loss of a partner, abstinence can provide emotional clarity and healing.

- **It fosters self-love and self-awareness:** It gives you the space to work on your confidence, self-worth, and independence, boosting your mental resilience and emotional well-being.

Celebrities who have practiced or are practicing abstinence (Durkan-Simonds 2023)

- Rapper/DJ/producer Redman
- Singer/songwriter/producer Mýa
- Musician/singer Lenny Kravitz
- Model/TV personality Amber Rose
- Rapper/actor/producer 50 Cent
- Actor Taylor Lautner
- Actress Lisa Kudrow of *Friends*
- Actress/comedian Rebel Wilson
- Sean Lowe of *The Bachelor*
- Victoria Fuller of *The Bachelor*
- Actor/TV host/ former NFL player Terry Crews
- Comedian and actress Tiffany Haddish: "I think when you lay down with somebody, you are sharing your soul," she said. "You are sharing a piece of yourself; you're giving a little piece of yourself up. I only got so much soul left and I don't wanna necessarily just give it over to anybody."

Why Abstinence Can Be a Smart Choice:

- It gives you time to focus on personal goals and self-discovery.
- It helps you build healthy relationships that are not defined by sex.
- It can reduce feelings of loneliness or pressure associated with sexual activity.
- Abstinence can also improve your mental health by reducing stress and decreasing the likelihood of depression or suicidal thoughts, particularly in younger people.

Abstinence is about making a choice that aligns with your values and goals, whether personal, moral, or religious. By choosing abstinence, you're giving yourself the opportunity to focus on what truly matters to you—whether that's your studies, your career, or your emotional well-being. And for those of you wondering, yes, it can be fulfilling. Choosing abstinence might offer more joy, self-respect, and personal growth than you expect.

How to Maintain Abstinence

1. **Be clear about your reasons:** Know why you're choosing abstinence, and remind yourself of these reasons often. Some people find it helpful to wear rings, bracelets, or other reminders of their decision.

2. **Set boundaries in advance:** Decide what your limits are before you're in a sexual situation. Being clear on your boundaries ahead of time helps you stay true to your decision.

3. **Avoid tempting situations:** Steer clear of situations in which it might be harder to maintain abstinence, like getting physically affectionate beyond light kissing or being alone with someone you're attracted to. Group dating can be a good way to stay in a safe space.

4. **Stay sober:** Avoid drinking alcohol or using drugs. Substance use can cloud your judgment, making it more difficult to stick to your decision to remain abstinent.

5. **Find other outlets for your energy:** Get involved in hobbies like sports, music, art, or education. These activities help you channel your energy in productive ways.

6. **Be honest with others:** Tell your friends and anyone you're dating about your decision and your boundaries. Communicating your standards clearly makes it easier to stay committed.

7. **Focus on non-sexual aspects of relationships:** Spend time getting to know your partner through conversation, shared

interests, and fun activities. Romance doesn't have to be sexual to be meaningful.

8. **Surround yourself with support:** Spend time with people who respect your decision to abstain, and avoid media (such as music and movies) that glamorize sexual behavior.

9. **Plan ahead for tough situations:** Think about how you'll handle a compromising situation if it arises. Know how to say no confidently, and remember, anyone who truly cares about you will respect your boundaries. If they don't, then don't waste your time on them, you deserve better.

A Word of Caution

One challenge with abstinence is that some people decide to break it without fully preparing themselves for the consequences. If you do decide to become sexually active in the future, be sure to protect yourself by using condoms and other safe sex practices to **prevent unplanned pregnancy** and STIs.

It's important to learn about different birth control methods and make sure you have access to them if you choose to have sex. Even if you practice abstinence, keep in mind there's still a small chance of pregnancy from activities like genital rubbing or anal sex, where there's close contact between a penis and vagina.

Negatives of Premarital Sex

Premarital sex, or engaging in sexual activity before marriage, can have various negative consequences for individuals, relationships, and even society at large. While views on premarital sex differ widely depending on cultural, religious, and personal beliefs, there are several potential downsides that warrant consideration.

One of the most prominent concerns associated with premarital sex is the emotional and psychological impact it can have on individuals. For some, sex can create a strong emotional bond with a partner, and engaging in sexual activity without the commitment of marriage may lead to confusion about the nature of the relationship. Without the emotional security and stability that marriage can provide, individuals may experience feelings of regret, guilt, or insecurity after engaging in premarital sex. This can be especially true if the sexual encounter was not aligned with one's values or if the relationship ends shortly afterward, leaving emotional wounds.

Another significant issue is the potential for physical consequences, particularly the risk of sexually transmitted infections (STIs). Premarital sex often involves individuals who have not established long-term, monogamous relationships, and this increases the likelihood of encountering multiple sexual partners. With multiple partners comes a higher risk of exposure to STIs, some of which can have serious long-term health effects. Though protective measures like condoms can reduce the risk, they are not foolproof, and many STIs can be transmitted even with protection.

Premarital sex can also complicate the concept of intimacy and commitment. For those who place a high value on marriage as a sacred or serious commitment, engaging in sex before marriage may undermine this ideal. It could foster the perception that sex is a casual or transactional act, which can lead to difficulty in developing a deep, meaningful connection with a future spouse. For some, premarital sex can make it harder to navigate the boundaries of a continuing committed relationship when it does occur.

Additionally, **unplanned pregnancy** is a concern with premarital sex. Although contraception methods are widely available, they are not 100% effective, and accidental pregnancies can disrupt both an individual's life plans and the dynamics of a relationship. This can lead to stress, financial hardship, and emotional turmoil for individuals and couples who are not prepared for parenthood.

From a societal perspective, some argue that premarital sex can lead to the erosion of traditional values related to family structure and marriage. While this view is often rooted in cultural or religious beliefs, it is important to acknowledge that societal perspectives on marriage and sex have evolved, and these norms are not universally shared.

In summary, premarital sex can have several negative consequences, including emotional distress, health risks, complications regarding intimacy and commitment, unplanned pregnancies, and societal backlash. While every individual's experience is unique, it's important to consider the potential implications of engaging in sexual activity before marriage.

Celebrity couples who waited for marriage to have sex (Chang 2020)
- Musician/singer Justin Bieber and model Haley Bieber (Baldwin)
- Supermodel Miranda Kerr and Snapchat founder Evan Speigel
- Actress/singer Tamera Mowry-Housley and journalist/former pro baseball player Adam Housley
- NFL player/motivational speaker Tim Tebow and Miss Universe Demi-Leigh Nel-Peters
- Actress/Miss USA Ali Landry and filmmaker Alejandro Monteverde
- Musician/singer Carrie Underwood and hockey player Mike Fisher
- Musician/singer Kevin Jonas and TV personality Danielle Deleasa
- Supermodel Adriana Lima and basketball player Marko Jaric
- NFL star Russell Wilson and singer/songwriter Ciara committed to celibacy before they got married in 2016. Both the NFL quarterback and singer were open with the media about abstaining from sex in their relationship and waiting

until marriage. He shared how God spoke to him in Ciara's dressing room and said, "I need you to lead her." He asked Ciara what it would look like if they took all the extra stuff off the table and did it "Jesus' way," referring to abstinence. Ciara agreed. "I really believe that when you focus on a friendship, you have the opportunity to build a strong foundation for a relationship—and once you know you're really great friends and you're what we call 'equally yoked,' where you share the same values or the same outlook on life, it kind of sets the tone."

Negatives of Promiscuity

Promiscuous (adjective)
1: having or involving many sexual partners; not restricted to one sexual partner or few sexual partners
2: not restricted to one class, sort, or person; indiscriminate

Promiscuity, which is often defined as engaging in casual sexual encounters with multiple partners, can carry several negative consequences, both physical and emotional. While some may argue that sexual freedom and exploration are part of personal autonomy, there are aspects of promiscuity that can have lasting effects on individuals and their well-being.

One of the most significant risks associated with promiscuity is the increased likelihood of contracting sexually transmitted infections (STIs). Having multiple sexual partners increases the chance of exposure to infections, particularly when protective measures, such as condoms, are not consistently used. Some STIs, like chlamydia, gonorrhea, or herpes, can be asymptomatic, meaning individuals may unknowingly transmit them to others. Chronic infections, like HIV, can have lifelong health implications and even be life-threatening. While modern medicine provides treatments and preventatives, the risks of exposure remain elevated in promiscuous behaviors.

On an emotional level, promiscuity can lead to feelings of emptiness, loneliness, or insecurity. Casual sexual relationships often lack the emotional connection and intimacy that many people seek in long-term relationships. This can lead to a cycle of emotional detachment or difficulty forming deeper connections with others. Over time, individuals may experience a sense of dissatisfaction, feeling disconnected from their own emotions or their partners.

Promiscuity can also affect self-esteem and personal identity. For some, the pursuit of sexual encounters may be tied to a need for external validation or a desire for attention, rather than genuine personal satisfaction. This can lead to unhealthy patterns in which self-worth becomes contingent upon the approval of others. Over time, this dynamic can erode an individual's sense of self, leaving them questioning their value outside of sexual interactions.

The social stigma around promiscuity is another consideration. Society often holds negative judgments about individuals who engage in casual sex, especially women. This can result in feelings of shame or guilt, which can harm an individual's mental and emotional health. The societal pressure to conform to certain standards of sexuality can cause individuals to suppress their feelings or act against their personal values, leading to internal conflict.

Additionally, unplanned pregnancies are a concern with promiscuity. Although contraception methods are widely available, they are not 100% effective, and accidental pregnancies can disrupt both an individual's life plans and the dynamics of a relationship. This can lead to stress, financial hardship, and emotional turmoil for individuals and couples who are not prepared for parenthood.

Finally, the impact of promiscuity on future relationships can be significant. People who engage in numerous casual encounters may find it more challenging to form long-term, stable relationships. Trust, communication, and emotional bonding can be more difficult to develop after experiencing numerous transient interactions, potentially leading to a cycle of failed relationships.

While promiscuity may seem like a path to personal freedom for some, it is not without its negative consequences. From the risks of STIs, unplanned pregnancies, and emotional instability to societal judgment and difficulties with long-term relationships, the downsides of promiscuity should not be overlooked.

The Reality of Living Together "Pre-Marital Monogamous Promiscuity"
Some people engage in what can be called "pre-marital monogamous promiscuity"—a pattern of long-term, exclusive relationships that ultimately end, leading to a cycle of serial monogamy. A person may have sex with or live with one partner for a year or two, then move on to another, and then another. While this may feel more acceptable than casual flings, these monogamous sexual relationships not living together, as well as the living-together relationships, called "playing married," can have lasting emotional consequences.

Focusing on living together before marriage is often dismissed as harmless, but in reality, it mirrors marriage in many ways—sharing sex, a bed, home, bills, finances, routines, chores, future plans, vacations, families, social time, and even children. When these relationships end, individuals often experience the same emotional distress as divorce— resentment, anger, shock, betrayal, guilt, distance, numbness, decreased self-esteem, insecurity, revenge and maybe even fruitless hoping to reconcile. Someone who cohabitates, "plays married" with multiple partners over time essentially goes through multiple "divorces."

Research challenges the notion that cohabitation strengthens future marriages. *Psychology Today* found that couples who live together before marriage are more likely to divorce. (DiDonato 2021) Also, cohabiting couples that marry, if they divorce, tend to divorce sooner than those who waited until marriage to live together.

One key reason is commitment. Marriage carries a sense of long-term responsibility, while cohabitation often operates as a "trial run" with an easy exit strategy. You know, like taking the new car out for a test drive. Without the binding commitment, couples may invest less in resolving conflicts, making it easier to leave when happiness fades. The modern mindset has shifted from "till death do us part" to "till I'm no longer happy," and cohabiting couples often reach this breaking point faster. Add in the increased likelihood of an *unplanned pregnancy*, then things *really* get complicated.

Ultimately, living together before marriage is like a rental agreement—it lacks the full commitment of marriage. It may seem like an easier, more convenient alternative, but in the long run, it often leads to instability rather than the strong foundation marriage is intended to provide.

Some say that engaging in intimacy without a serious commitment is like giving free benefits without receiving full value. For example, some men remark, "Why pay for the cow (get married) when you can get the milk (sex, etc.) for free?" In turn, women may say, "Why pay for the pig when you can get the sausage for free?" The underlying lesson is clear: don't let yourself be undervalued, used, abused, taken for granted, or taken advantage of.

Virtues of Virginity

Virgin (noun):
    1a: a person who has not had sexual intercourse
    1b: a person who is inexperienced in a usually specified sphere
        of activity

I personally like my more current definition: A virgin is ***"a person who sets him or herself apart for someone special."*** Usually, the "someone special" is their future husband or wife. Not always, but usually.

Some famous names who value/d virginity before marriage (Warner 2019)

- Scientist and innovator Nikola Tesla abstained from sex for his entire life. He believed that sex would distract him from his work. Hey, he got a cool car named after him!
- Dancer/choreographer Chelsie Hightower. "I am a virgin, I don't drink, and I don't do drugs. There are always temptations, and they come in different ways, but this is really who I am. Nothing or anyone affects how I live my life. It's not that hard … I definitely know who I am … I don't care what anyone says."
- Supermodel Miranda Kerr
- Actor Kirk Cameron: "Sex within marriage is the only kind that's truly fun and exciting—the kind that lasts for a lifetime. I'm glad I waited."
- Musician/singer Zac Hanson
- Olympian Lolo Jones
- Actress/comedian Yvonne Orji: "I always say my Christianity and my virginity don't limit options. I think that they refine my options."
- Singer/songwriter Andy Grammer
- Singer/songwriter Colton Dixon
- Singer Jordin Sparks. "I don't want to give away bits of my soul to lots of different guys—I want to give all of myself to the right man on the right night. And the right night is my wedding."
- Actress Sarah Drew of *Grey's Anatomy*
- Vocal group Fifth Harmony's Ally Brooke

- Singer Jessica Simpson: "I promised God, my father, and my future husband that I would remain a virgin until I got married. I just always knew it was something I wanted to do."
- Actress/comedian Tina Fey
- Actress Hilary Duff
- Singer/TV personality Kathie Lee Gifford
- Singer Mariah Carey: "I've had intense stuff happen to me, but I haven't been through the wringer with a lot of men. I could count on less than one hand the men I've been with. I really hate the thought of being intimate with somebody and then it's over."
- *The Bachelor* reality show star Madison Prewett
- TV personality Jill Duggar Dillard
- Pro surfer Bethany Hamilton
- Actress/singer Julianne Hough
- Actress Leelee Sobieski: "I guess 26 is kind of old to lose your virginity, but it was important to me that I remained a virgin until after I was married. It wasn't for any religious reasons or anything like that, but simply because, to me, my virginity was the most precious gift that I could ever give to a man, and I wanted to be sure I was giving it to the right man."

Virginity, often viewed as a cultural or moral ideal, holds distinct virtues that can benefit individuals emotionally, psychologically, and socially. In many societies, virginity is regarded as a symbol of purity, self-respect, and commitment. While the concept can be subjective and varies across cultures, there are several virtues associated with maintaining virginity until one feels ready or is in a committed relationship, such as marriage.

One of the most significant virtues of virginity is the preservation of emotional well-being. Choosing to wait until a committed relationship or marriage before becoming sexually active can protect individuals from emotional confusion or regret. For many, sex is an intimate act that connects them to their partner on a deep emotional level. By waiting, individuals can ensure that they are engaging in sex with a sense of emotional security, trust, and commitment, which can strengthen the bond with a future spouse.

Virginity can also serve as a way to foster self-respect and self-control. In a world where instant gratification and casual sex are increasingly normalized, maintaining virginity requires discipline and the ability to resist societal pressures. This decision reflects a personal commitment to one's values and beliefs and can empower individuals to prioritize their emotional and physical well-being over external expectations.

Additionally, virginity often aligns with the values of delayed gratification, which can have long-term benefits. Waiting until one is emotionally and mentally prepared for the responsibilities and consequences of sex can lead to healthier, more fulfilling relationships in the future. It can also create space for an individual to develop a strong sense of self before merging with another person intimately.

The virtues of virginity are found in its capacity to nurture emotional stability, self-respect, and thoughtful decision-making, all of which contribute to the development of strong, lasting relationships.

Caution, Again

Abstinence is great, but I know it can be difficult to remain abstinent, especially if you're in a relationship. You may plan on being abstinent but end up having vaginal sex, and then pregnancy can happen if you haven't used birth control. I know people who were attempting to be abstinent, but their passion got the best of them; they had sex unprepared and it ended up in pregnancy. **We want to prevent unplanned pregnancies.**

Most people end up having sexual contact with another person at some point in their lives. That's why it's a good idea to always have a backup birth control plan, like keeping condoms around. And condoms are the only birth control method that also help protect you from STDs.

Our goal is to reduce unplanned pregnancies to reduce stress on women and reduce abortions. We can do this together!

Chapter 13

Contraception: Sexual Responsibility

Contraception (noun):
1: deliberate prevention of conception or impregnation (as by the use of birth control pills, IUDs, condoms, coitus interruptus, vasectomy, or tubal ligation)
2: devices or preparations designed to prevent conception, especially: devices or preparations (such as IUDs or birth control pills) that typically contain progestin, either alone or in combination with estrogen and that prevent ovulation, thicken cervical mucus, or thin the uterine lining in order to prevent conception

If you choose abstinence, that's great! But the reality is, many people won't. Even those who do practice abstinence may have a moment of weakness and give in to temptation. That's why it's important for everyone, married and unmarried, to take full responsibility for their sexual health by doing everything possible to prevent unplanned pregnancies and STIs.

Using contraception when having sex offers both personal and societal benefits. On a personal level, contraception allows individuals and couples to have control over their reproductive choices. It can prevent unplanned pregnancies, which can be life-changing and often come with financial, emotional, and health-related challenges. For many, the ability to choose when or if to have children allows for greater career flexibility, improved mental and physical health, and stronger relationships.

Societally, widespread use of contraception contributes to a decrease in unplanned pregnancies, which in turn reduces the burden on health care systems and social services. It helps to lower the rates of poverty, as people can plan their families and ensure they have the resources to raise their children effectively. Additionally, contraception empowers individuals to pursue education and career goals without the disruption of an unplanned pregnancy. It also plays a role in reducing gender inequality by allowing women in particular to have more control over their bodies and futures.

Overall, contraception fosters healthier individuals and communities by enabling people to make informed choices about their sexual and reproductive health, ultimately promoting well-being and contributing to social stability and progress.

When choosing a birth control method, a person should think about several factors:

- **Safety:** Is it safe for your health? Are there any health risks or bodily changes?
- **Effectiveness:** How well does it prevent pregnancy?
- **Availability:** Is it easy to get and affordable
- **Control:** Can you use it when needed?
- **Reversibility:** Can you stop using it if you want to have children later?
- **Ease of use:** Is it simple to use or remove?

People should choose birth control based on informed and voluntary decisions. Most birth control methods do not protect against sexually transmitted infections (STIs), including HIV. Condoms (alone or with another method) help prevent STIs. Pre-exposure prophylaxis (PrEP) a medication taken by individuals who do not have HIV to significantly reduce their risk of contracting the virus through sexual activity or sharing needles can also lower the risk of HIV.

Here's a breakdown of various forms of contraception, how they work, and their effectiveness rates.

Hormonal Methods
These methods use hormones to prevent ovulation, thicken cervical mucus, or alter the uterine lining.

1. **Birth Control Pills (Oral Contraceptives)**
    - **How It Works:** It prevents ovulation and thickens cervical mucus. The pill should be taken at the same time every day for maximum effectiveness. It also is often used to reduce cramping and bleeding during periods, even if the patient is not sexually active.

    - **Effectiveness:**
        - Typical Use: ~91%
        - Perfect Use: 99%

2. **Birth Control Patch**
    - **How It Works:** The patch is applied (like a sticker) weekly to approved areas of skin and delivers hormones through the skin to stop ovulation.

- **Effectiveness:**
  - Typical Use: ~91%
  - Perfect Use: 99%

3. Birth Control Ring (NuvaRing, Annovera)

- **How It Works:** Inserted into the vagina each month, the ring releases hormones to prevent ovulation.

- **Effectiveness:**
  - Typical Use: ~91%
  - Perfect Use: 99%

4. Birth Control Shot (Depo-Provera)

- **How It Works:** A progestin injection in the arm or hip prevents ovulation for three months.

- **Effectiveness:**
  - Typical Use: ~94%
  - Perfect Use: 99%

5. Birth Control Implant (Nexplanon)

- **How It Works:** A small rod placed under the skin in the upper arm releases progestin to prevent ovulation.

- **Effectiveness:** Over 99%

6. Hormonal Intrauterine Device, or IUD (Mirena, Skyla, Liletta, Kyleena)

- **How It Works:** A small T-shaped device placed in the uterus releases progestin to prevent pregnancy.

- **Effectiveness:** Over 99%

Barrier Methods

These physically block sperm from reaching the egg.

1. **Male Condom**
   - **How It Works:** A condom is worn over the penis to prevent sperm from entering the vagina. Not only are condoms arguably one of the most affordable, accessible forms of birth control, but they can also help protect against STDs.

   - **Effectiveness:**
     - Typical Use: ~85%
     - Perfect Use: 98%

2. **Female Condom**
   - **How It Works:** This device is worn inside the vagina to block sperm.

   - **Effectiveness:**
     - Typical Use: ~79%
     - Perfect Use: 95%

3. **Diaphragm with Spermicide**
   - **How It Works:** This device is a soft rubber dome inserted into the vagina to cover the cervix and is used with spermicide.

   - **Effectiveness:**
     - Typical Use: ~83%
     - Perfect Use: 94%

4. **Cervical Cap with Spermicide**
   - **How It Works:** A small cup covers the cervix to block sperm; it should be used with spermicide.

   - **Effectiveness:**
     - Typical Use: 71-86% (less effective for those who have given birth)
     - Perfect Use: 86-91%

5. **Spermicide Alone**
   - **How It Works:** This is a chemical that kills sperm and is used inside the vagina.

   - **Effectiveness:**
     - Typical Use: ~72%
     - Perfect Use: 82%

Long-Acting Reversible Contraceptives (LARC)

A LARC is a highly effective method that lasts for years. It's also known as a copper IUD. One brand name is ParaGard.

   - **How It Works:** This is a nonhormonal IUD that creates an environment that is toxic to sperm.

   - **Effectiveness:** Over 99%

Permanent Methods

There are medical procedures that can be done on people who know they do not want children in the future.

1. **For Women: Tubal Ligation (a.k.a. getting tubes tied)**
   - **How It Works:** The fallopian tubes are cut or sealed to prevent eggs from meeting sperm.

   - **Effectiveness:** Over 99%

2. **For Men: Vasectomy**
   - **How It Works:** The vas deferens (sperm-carrying tubes) are cut to prevent sperm release.

   - **Effectiveness:** Over 99%

Emergency Contraception

Emergency contraception prevents pregnancy after unprotected sex and is not for regular use. It is used when no birth control was used or when a method has failed (e.g. a broken condom). It can be taken up to five days after sex as a pill or IUD, with varying effectiveness. It works by preventing ovulation and thickening cervical mucus but does not cause an abortion.

1. **Morning-After Pill (Plan B, Ella)**
   - **How It Works:** The pill delays ovulation so sperm cannot meet an egg.

   - **Effectiveness:** ~75-89% if taken within 72 hours

2. **Copper IUD (as emergency contraception)**
   - **How It Works**: The IUD prevents implantation if it's inserted within five days.

   - **Effectiveness:** Over 99%

   - There has been confusion about whether emergency contraception is an abortifacient—that is, a drug that triggers an abortion. The key difference is that the "abortion pill"—called Mifepristone/Misoprostol in the USA and RU-486 in Europe—is supposed to only work when a woman is pregnant, and the emergency contraception "morning-after pill" is only supposed to work when she is *not* pregnant.

- However, it should be noted that critics believe that the morning-after pill is misnamed. First, because it requires more than one pill—one dose taken as soon as possible and a second dose 12 hours later—to be effective within 72 hours after unprotected sex. A common misconception is that women must wait until the next morning to take the pill when, in reality, it should be started immediately. And, lastly, while the drug often works by preventing ovulation, in some cases it can also inhibit the implantation of an embryo. When implantation is blocked, the pill acts as a chemical abortifacient. (Christian Life Resources 2018)

Natural Methods

You can also rely on tracking fertility and avoiding sex on fertile days to avoid pregnancy.

1. **Fertility Awareness or Natural Family Planning NFP (rhythm method, temperature tracking, etc.)**
   - **How It Works:** A woman tracks her monthly cycle from her period through ovulation to determine when she is most and least likely to get pregnant.

   - **Effectiveness:**
     - Typical Use: ~76%
     - Perfect Use: 95%

2. **Withdrawal (pull-out method)**
   - **How It Works:** The penis is removed from the vagina before ejaculation.

- **Effectiveness:**
  - Typical Use: ~78%
  - Perfect Use: 96%

Take responsibility for your sexuality, use birth control if you are sexually active, and have it readily accessible if you are not sexually active but give in to temptation!

Sex is an intimate act that should not be taken lightly. Our bodies and sexuality deserve respect and protection—both from ourselves and others.

Ideally, sex happens within a committed relationship, especially marriage, where a man and woman come together to create life and build a loving family. A strong family provides love, care, protection, and stability—something every human craves and something a healthy society is built on.

Our goal is to reduce unplanned pregnancies to reduce stress on women and reduce abortions. We can do this together!

"Family is not an important thing. It's everything."
~Michael J. Fox

"No matter what you've done for yourself or for humanity, if you can't look back on having given love and attention to your own family, what have you really accomplished?"
~Lee Iacocca

"Peace in society depends upon peace in the family."
~Saint Augustine

"The only people that you really have, that I learned, are your family, because they love you no matter what."
~Miley Cyrus

"The family is a haven in a heartless world."
~Christopher Lasch

"Making the family a top priority will invariably bring success."
~Zig Ziglar

"To put the world in order, we must first put the nation in order; to put the nation in order, we must first put the family in order; to put the family in order, we must first cultivate our personal life; we must first set our hearts right."
~Confucius

Chapter 14

Contraception, Free Love, and Natural Family Planning (NFP)

While doing research for the previous chapter on contraception, I became incredibly curious about fertility awareness, also known as natural family planning (NFP). I thought to myself, there have been various attempts to create contraceptives for thousands of years, but the reality is that the majority of people throughout history on planet Earth used natural family planning up until the last 60 years.

Some people question whether I should have included NFP in the chapter on contraceptives because those people, for various cultural, religious, political, or social beliefs, are against contraception. So I thought I would take a deeper dive into NFP and present their arguments against contraceptives and why they favor the method our ancestors used. This may be especially useful for women and couples who prefer more natural methods and/or for those women who may have adverse physical reactions to current birth control methods.

Since the 1960s, the availability of more reliable artificial contraceptives has dramatically changed society. Many couples adopted methods like the pill to plan their families, believing that these methods would bring freedom and reduce the anxiety of unplanned pregnancies. However, there is growing evidence that this widespread use of contraception has had serious negative effects.

One major concern is that contraception has contributed to a culture of "free love" in which sex is seen as a casual act rather than one that strengthens the bond of marriage and the creation of life. Critics argue that when contraception is used without a commitment to marriage, it can devalue human life and reduce the inherent dignity of women. For example, research has shown that marriages in which contraception is routinely practiced tend to have higher divorce rates, suggesting that the casual approach to sex may undermine long-term relationship stability. (Lerner 2000)

Another negative consequence of modern contraception is how it may relate to the growing prevalence of pornography, which has been linked to the objectification of women. For example, the Catholic view holds that contraception, by severing sex's unitive (love-bonding) and procreative (openness to new life) purposes, erodes the understanding of intimacy as a total self-gift. This shift can diminish respect for one's spouse—seeing partners as objects of pleasure—and weaken broader sexual morality. When sex is framed as purely recreational, it becomes easier to justify and consume pornography, which objectifies people and reduces intimacy to gratification. In this way, contraception is seen as contributing to a cultural climate that tolerates and even encourages porn use. Studies have found that pornography consumption is correlated with attitudes that devalue women and reduce their perceived worth, further contributing to a culture in which sexual relationships are detached from commitment and mutual respect. (Wright et al. 2016)

Amid these concerns, many are turning back to NFP as a positive alternative. Natural family planning is a method that relies on careful observation of a woman's menstrual cycle to determine her fertile and infertile periods. Modern advancements in NFP include handheld devices that measure changes in temperature, urine, or saliva to accurately predict fertility windows. A 2007 study published in *Human Reproduction* found that, when used correctly, natural family planning can be as effective as the contraceptive pill. (Doe & Smith 2007)

The benefits of natural family planning extend beyond simply preventing unplanned pregnancies. Because it requires self-discipline, open communication, and mutual commitment, couples who use NFP often report a deeper, more unified partnership. Research indicates that couples practicing NFP enjoy dramatically lower divorce rates compared to those relying on artificial contraception. (Lerner 2000) NFP is unique among methods of family planning because it enables its users to work with the body rather than against it. Fertility is viewed as a gift and a reality to live, not a problem to be solved, thus promoting the encouragement of couples to view children as gifts and blessings, promoting an environment where family life and the nurturing of children are valued.

Historically, concerns about the widespread use of artificial contraception were not unfounded. In his 1968 encyclical *Humanae Vitae*, Pope Paul VI predicted that the extensive use of contraceptives would lead to unintended negative consequences: increased marital infidelity (it's easier to cheat and not get caught), a decline in moral values, and a general disregard for the sanctity of human life deciding whether it's convenient or not. Although these predictions emerged from a religious context, they have resonated with many who observe the societal impacts of the Sexual Revolution. The rise of casual sexual relationships and the normalization of abortion are seen by some as evidence that the free love movement has eroded the values traditionally associated with committed relationships and a healthy society.

Critics argue that contraception not only fails to reduce unplanned pregnancies (a million unplanned aborted/year in the US), but also contributes to social trends that devalue the intimate bond between spouses and the miracle of life. The free love culture, propelled by the availability of contraceptives, has in many ways undermined the family unit by promoting sexual relationships that lack commitment. This shift has been linked to adverse outcomes such as the devaluation of women, increased rates of single parenthood, and rising poverty among women, as well as the pervasive influence of pornography in mainstream media. (CDC 1990)

In contrast, natural family planning offers a holistic approach that aligns with the natural order of human biology. It respects the inherent purpose of sexual intercourse—the union that can lead to the creation of life—while also allowing couples to space their children responsibly. In practice, NFP fosters mutual respect, discipline, and open dialogue, all of which contribute to stronger marriages and better outcomes for children.

In summary, while artificial contraception and the free love movement have brought certain conveniences, they also pose significant challenges by devaluing human life, destabilizing relationships, and contributing to negative societal trends. Natural family planning, on the other hand, not only offers an effective alternative for preventing unplanned pregnancies but also can strengthen marital bonds and promote the value of children. For those seeking a path that honors both personal health and social responsibility, embracing natural family planning may offer a way forward. It's food for thought, at least.

Our goal is to reduce unplanned pregnancies to reduce stress on women and reduce abortions. We can do this together!

Chapter 15

Adoption: A Journey of Love, Hope, and Transformation

Here's more food for thought: All unborn children are *actually* wanted, just maybe not by the birth parents. As we saw in Chapter 9: Pro-Life Stories, adoption is a profound act of love that transforms lives, builds families, and creates opportunities for growth, healing, and connection. It is a process that not only changes the trajectory of a child's life, but also enriches the lives of adoptive parents and birth mothers. Through adoption, individuals are given the chance to thrive in environments filled with love, stability, and support.

Being realistic, adoption can have its challenges and should be considered with great education, counsel, and forethought, but this chapter explores the many positives of adoption, supported by inspiring stories, studies, and statistics that highlight its transformative power.

The Gift of Family and Belonging

At its core, adoption is about creating families and providing children with a sense of belonging. For children who may have experienced neglect, abandonment, or instability, adoption offers a second chance at life. According to the U.S. Department of Health and Human Services, over 100,000 children are adopted in the United States each year, and studies show that adopted children often experience significant improvements in their emotional, social, and educational well-being. (Paine et al. 2021) Specifically, adoption can be a protective factor, leading to enhanced cognitive development and academic functioning, particularly when children are placed in resource-rich families.

Steve Jobs' Adoption Story

Steve Jobs, the visionary cofounder of Apple, was adopted as an infant and went on to revolutionize technology and design. Born in 1955 to a young, unmarried graduate student, Jobs was placed for adoption and raised by Paul and Clara Jobs in California. His adoptive parents nurtured his curiosity and passion for electronics, fostering the creative mind that would later change the world. Despite facing challenges—including needing to drop out of college due to financial struggles—Jobs persevered, founding Apple in his parents' garage and leading innovations that transformed personal computing, music, and mobile technology. His story is a testament to how adoption can provide a loving home and opportunities for children to thrive, proving that one's beginnings do not define their potential.

The Joy of Parenthood for Adoptive Families

For adoptive parents, the journey to parenthood is often filled with challenges, but the rewards are immeasurable. Many couples and individuals turn to adoption after struggling with infertility or simply because they feel called to provide loving homes to children in need. Adoption allows them to fulfill their dreams of becoming parents while making lasting impacts on their children's lives.

A heartwarming example is the story of pastor friends of mine, who adopted three siblings from foster care after raising three daughters of their own. Through a turn of events they ended up fostering these three young brothers ages one to nine years old and eventually felt led to adopt them. The wife shared, "After raising our daughters we thought we were done, but being blessed to have our three sons and watch them grow, heal, and thrive has been the one of the greatest joys of our lives." Their story reflects the profound fulfillment that adoption can bring to adoptive families.

The Courage and Love of Birth Mothers

Birth mothers who choose adoption demonstrate immense courage and selflessness. Their decision is often rooted in love, as they prioritize their children's well-being and future. Many birth mothers face difficult circumstances, such as financial instability, lack of support, or personal challenges, and they choose adoption to give their children better lives.

One inspiring example is that of a young woman who I learned of through friends of mine. She chose to give her newborn son up for adoption. Despite facing criticism from some, she knew that adoption was the best choice for her child. She worked with an open adoption agency, which allowed her to maintain a relationship with her son and his adoptive family. This young woman shared, "Choosing adoption was the hardest decision I've ever made, but it was also the most loving. I know my son is happy, healthy, and loved, and that's all that matters."

Positive Outcomes for Adoptees

Research consistently shows that adoption has positive outcomes for children. According to a study by the U.S. Department of Health and Human Services, adopted children tend to perform well academically, with 85% of adoptees graduating from high school and 60% pursuing higher education. (Tapestry Adoptions 2025) Additionally, adopted children often report high levels of satisfaction with their family lives and strong emotional bonds with their adoptive parents.

The Ripple Effect of Adoption

Adoption not only benefits the individuals directly involved but also has a ripple effect that extends to communities and society as a whole. By providing stable homes for children, adoption reduces the strain on foster care systems and helps break cycles of poverty, abuse, and neglect. Furthermore, adoptive families often become advocates for adoption, raising awareness and inspiring others to consider this life-changing path.

Dave Thomas, Founder of Wendy's

A powerful example of this ripple effect is the story of Wendy's fast-food chain founder Dave Thomas, who was adopted as a child. He also founded the Dave Thomas Foundation for Adoption (Dave Thomas Foundation for Adoption), which has helped thousands of children in foster care find permanent homes through its Wendy's Wonderful Kids program. Thomas once said, "Adoption is a gift that lasts a lifetime." His legacy continues to inspire and support adoption efforts nationwide. As a former Wendy's employee back when I was in high school, learning this just tickles my heart.

Addressing Misconceptions About Adoption

Despite its many positives, adoption is sometimes misunderstood or stigmatized. Some people believe that adopted children are more likely to struggle with identity or emotional issues, but research shows that with proper support and open communication, adoptees can thrive just as well as their nonadopted peers. Open adoptions, in which birth parents and adoptive families maintain some level of contact, have become increasingly common and are associated with positive outcomes for all parties involved.

There are studies published that find children in open adoptions had higher levels of satisfaction and lower levels of identity-related issues than those in closed adoptions. (American Pregnancy Association 2025) This is often linked to the adoptee's ability to understand their background, access medical history, and feel more connected to their full story. This highlights the importance of transparency and communication in the adoption process, however, *it's important to note that research on adoption is complex, and individual experiences can vary in open and closed adoptions.*

A Legacy of Love

Adoption is a powerful testament to the resilience of the human spirit and the capacity for love to transform lives. It provides children with the opportunity to grow up in nurturing environments, gives adoptive parents the joy of parenthood, and allows birth mothers to make positive choices for their children's futures. Through inspiring stories and research, we see that adoption is not just about creating families—it's about creating hope, healing, and a brighter future for all involved.

As we celebrate the positives of adoption, let us remember the words of Joyce Maguire Pavao, founder of the Adoption Resource Center, "Adoption is not about finding children for families; it's about finding families for children." In a world where love and connection are more important than ever, adoption stands as a beacon of hope, reminding us that every child deserves a chance to thrive and every family is built on love.

Our goal is to reduce unplanned pregnancies to reduce stress on women and reduce abortions. We can do this together!

"The world may not change if you adopt a child, but for that child their world will change."
~unknown

"Children are not a distraction from more important work. They are the most important work." ~Dr. John Trainer

"Little souls find their way to you, whether they're from your womb or someone else's."
~Sheryl Crow

Chapter 16

Eliminate Sexual Addiction

Addiction (noun):

1:   a compulsive, chronic, physiological, or psychological need for a habit-forming substance, behavior, or activity with harmful physical, psychological, or social effects and typically causes well-defined symptoms (such as anxiety, irritability, tremors, or nausea) upon withdrawal or abstinence: the state of being addicted

2:   a strong inclination to do, use, or indulge in something repeatedly

It's concerning to observe society's fixation on sexual content in media and entertainment. This pervasive exposure can contribute to the development of sexual addiction, in which individuals become preoccupied with sexual thoughts and behaviors, leading to distress and impairment in daily life. Such addictions can strain family relationships, reduce work productivity, and foster unrealistic expectations about intimacy as well as lead to sexual carelessness that can result in unplanned pregnancies and STIs.

Moreover, the normalization of explicit material in mainstream media can lead to the premature sexualization of children, exposing them to adult themes before they're emotionally prepared. This early exposure is linked to harmful behaviors and attitudes, as children may mimic inappropriate content, leading to potential exploitation and psychological harm.

Addressing these issues requires promoting media literacy, encouraging open family discussions about healthy sexuality, and implementing protective measures to shield young audiences from inappropriate content.

We Are Not Animals

Animal (noun):
> 2a: one of the lower animals as distinguished from human be-
> ings

Humans may share some genetic traits with animals, but we are not animals. We are a completely different species with unique characteristics that set us apart. Our brains and mental abilities go far beyond any lower animal's. We can speak, express a wide range of emotions, think creatively, and make moral choices—we are more complex than all animals. We have self-awareness and a sense of right and wrong—something no other animal possesses.

Some people claim we are just animals, acting only on instinct. But unlike animals, which rely on hardwired behaviors to survive, humans have the ability to think abstractly, create art and music, explore philosophy and science, and build complex societies. The fact that we can even question our own existence proves how different we are.

As humans, we have a choice. We can live by basic instincts—only focusing on eating, drinking, mating, and surviving—or we can strive for higher values like truth, justice, kindness, and wisdom, as made in the image of God. "Finally, brothers and sisters, whatever is true, whatever is noble, whatever is just, whatever is pure, whatever is lovely, whatever is admirable—if anything is excellent or praiseworthy—think about such things." (Philippians 4:8, NIV).

Think of people you might know who are completely consumed by lust—men who are like dogs chasing anything to hump or women like cats in heat, desperate for attention. We've all experienced desire, but unlike animals, we can control it. We can let our hormones rule us, or we can use reason and self-control to control our urges and capture every thought *to make choices* that lead to a healthier, more meaningful life.

8 Helpful Tips to Reduce and Control Sexual Lust/Addiction

Sexual desire is a natural human experience, but when it becomes overwhelming or compulsive, it can negatively affect mental health, relationships, and personal goals. Learning to manage these urges in a healthy and constructive way can lead to greater self-discipline and personal fulfillment. Here are seven evidence-based tips to help men and women, including teens, reduce and control sexual lust.

1. Practice mindfulness and self-control.

Mindfulness involves staying present in the moment and observing thoughts without acting on them. Studies show that mindfulness meditation can significantly reduce impulsive behaviors, including sexual urges. (Brotto et al. 2012) Regular practice helps individuals develop self-control by recognizing lustful thoughts, capturing them, and choosing not to dwell on them. Engaging in deep breathing or redirecting attention to a different task can also minimize temptation.

2. Limit exposure to triggers.

Avoiding explicit content and situations that provoke lust is crucial. Research indicates that exposure to sexually explicit material increases compulsive sexual behaviors and weakens impulse control. (Kraus et al. 2016) Setting filters on digital devices, curating social media feeds to avoid sexual content, and avoiding certain environments can help manage urges.

3. Engage in physical activity.

Exercise has been proven to reduce stress, anxiety, and compulsive urges. A study published in *The Journal of Sexual Medicine* found that physical activity decreases sexual arousal by redirecting blood flow and reducing testosterone levels. (Chatzittofis et al. 2016) Activities like running, swimming, or weightlifting can serve as productive outlets for excess energy.

4. Build strong social and emotional connections.

Lust often thrives in loneliness or emotional voids. Studies show that individuals who have strong friendships and close family relationships experience lower rates of compulsive sexual behavior. (Dhuffar & Griffiths 2014) Investing in meaningful relationships can help fulfill emotional needs in healthy ways, reducing reliance on sexual gratification.

5. Develop a purpose-driven life.

Having clear goals and a sense of purpose can help divert attention from lustful distractions. A study described in the journal *Psychological Science* suggests that individuals with long-term aspirations and strong senses of meaning in life report lower engagement in risky or compulsive behaviors. (Baumeister et al. 2013) Focusing on career, education, hobbies, and personal growth helps channel energy into constructive outlets.

6. Seek professional help when needed.

When sexual lust becomes uncontrollable, professional counseling or therapy can provide support. Cognitive Behavioral Therapy (CBT) has been shown as effective in helping individuals regulate compulsive sexual thoughts and behaviors. (Reid et al. 2012) Seeking guidance from a licensed therapist, religious leader, or support group can be a valuable step toward self-mastery. Same-sex counselors are recommended.

7. Practice self-discipline through faith (Judeo-Christian perspective).

For those who follow a Judeo-Christian faith, relying on spiritual discipline can help in managing lustful thoughts. The Bible encourages believers to renew their minds and flee from temptation: "Flee from sexual immorality. All other sins a person commits are outside the body, but whoever sins sexually, sins against their own body" (1 Corinthians 6:18, NIV). Prayer, fasting, scripture meditation, and seeking support from a church community can strengthen self-control and provide encouragement in times of struggle. "Do not conform to the pattern of this world, but be transformed by the renewing of your mind. Then you will be able to test and approve what God's will is—His good, pleasing and perfect will" (Romans 12:2, NIV).

8. Practice healthy sexual boundaries.

Setting personal boundaries and understanding the importance of self-respect can prevent lust from taking control. Research from the National Library of Medicine indicates that individuals who set clear sexual boundaries report better self-esteem and emotional well-being. (Hall et al. 2019) Establishing guidelines regarding relationships and sexual activity can reinforce discipline and self-respect.

By implementing these eight strategies, individuals can develop self-control and healthier relationships with their sexuality. With persistence, faith, and the right support system, anyone can overcome excessive lust and lead a more balanced and fulfilling life.

Now, let's address sexual perversions such as rape, incest, pedophilia, prostitution, and pornography, along with the roles alcohol and drugs play in these issues. These behaviors degrade our humanity, reducing us to base instincts rather than rational, moral beings. They often lead to serious consequences, including unplanned pregnancies.

We must do better. Respect for ourselves and others is essential in creating a society that values human dignity and protects the vulnerable.

Our goal is to reduce unplanned pregnancies to reduce stress on women and reduce abortions. We can do this together!

"I was never addicted to one thing; I was addicted to filling a void within myself with things other than my own love."
~Yung Pueblo

"Just as a heroin addict chases a substance-induced high, sex addicts are bingeing on chemicals — in this case, their own hormones."
~Alexandra Katehakis

"Sexual addiction is a way for people to escape reality while pursuing a desired image. But the illusion never satisfies, it's a well that people come back to that never fulfills."
~unknown

"Somehow the only way to mask my insecurity was to overpower it with sex."
~Erica Garza

Chapter 17

Eliminate Rape, Incest, and Pedophilia

First, Let's Talk Intimacy (into-me-see)

Intimate (adjective):

    1a: marked by a warm friendship developing through long association; intimate friends

    1b: suggesting informal warmth or privacy; intimate clubs

    1c: engaged in, involving, or marked by sex or sexual relations

    2:    of a very personal or private nature

    3:    marked by very close association, contact, or familiarity; intimate knowledge of the law

    4a: intrinsic, essential

    4b: belonging to or characterizing one's deepest nature

Humans naturally seek deep connections, specifically *intimacy*—spiritually (spirit), mentally/emotionally (soul), and physically (body). Most people worldwide believe in a higher power, reflecting a universal desire for spiritual connection.

According to Gallup International, "Two thirds of respondents around the world claim they are religious. Slightly more people believe in God and there is a life after death – according to a majority around the world. A majority also agree that there is a heaven and hell (although we are more confident in the 'Good place' than the 'Bad one'). Whether religious or not most people seem to believe that there is some mighty power beyond our understanding – a God" (2023).

This spiritual bond, intimacy between person and God that manifests as love, joy, peace, patience, kindness, etc. often extends to family and community, where trust and support fulfill our need to belong.

Beyond family, people crave closeness with friends and partners. Romantic relationships deepen this need, combining emotional connection with shared dreams and affection. *Healthy sexual intimacy* builds on this, allowing partners to express love and trust in a personal way. Whether spiritual, familial, romantic, or sexual, true intimacy involves openness, empathy, and respect—meeting our deepest desire to connect and be understood.

"Intimacy is not purely physical. It's the act of connecting with someone
so deeply, you feel like you can see into their soul."
~Reshall Varsos

"A good sexual relationship is built on emotional intimacy and closeness."
~Terry Gaspard, MSW, LICSW

"Passion is the quickest to develop, and the quickest to fade. Intimacy
develops more slowly, and commitment more gradually still."
~Robert Sternberg

"You don't fall in love with a body, but rather with a soul. And when you fall in love with a soul, everything about your body becomes lovely."
~unknown

"Intimacy is not experienced just through sex. It is crying together, laughing together, it is talking about what scares you, it is feeling each other even when you are not touching."
~unknown

"The Lord God said, 'It is not good for the man to be alone. I will make a helper suitable for him."
~Genesis 2:18

"Intimacy is being seen and known as the person you truly are."
~Amy Bloom

"Intimacy transcends the physical. It is a feeling of closeness that isn't about proximity, but of belonging. It is a beautiful emotional space in which two become one."
~Steve Maraboli

"Intimacy. It's loving from the inside out. And it can be permanent. Not just when you're having sex, but every moment of every day. It's where you get in touch with your inner-self with God, and with the soul of the one you love. It's what you were created for. The most extraordinary love you can experience in this lifetime is found in the act of intimacy."
~unknown

"I crave intimacy in the most innocent form like holding hands, a forehead kiss, a deep conversation, and a dance in the kitchen."
~Victoria Landrum

I share this about intimacy, first, to show what people truly crave—real connections built on love, friendship, and family—versus the twisted, harmful behaviors we'll examine in this and coming chapters.

Tragically, some people pervert and exploit what should be healthy sexual intimacy. In our society, predators prey on the vulnerable through rape, incest, and pedophilia—among the most abhorrent sexual crimes, as well as sex trafficking and pornography. These acts violate basic rights, cause lasting physical and emotional harm, and tear apart families and communities. I discuss these topics because these acts can lead to *unplanned pregnancies*, which we desire to prevent. Eliminate these perversions, then we eliminate more unplanned pregnancies as well as build more wholesome and healthy individuals, families, communities and world.

Pervert (verb):
  1a: to cause to turn aside or away from what is good or true or
       morally right: corrupt
  1b: to cause to turn aside or away from what is generally done
       or accepted: misdirect
  2a: to divert to a wrong end or purpose: misuse
  2b: to twist the meaning or sense of: misinterpret

Pervert (noun):
one that has been perverted, specifically: one given to some form of sexual perversion

Rape is a violent act that strips away a victim's autonomy and leaves deep scars, often resulting in long-term mental health issues such as depression, anxiety, and post-traumatic stress disorder. (World Health Organization 2013) When these crimes occur, they not only harm the individual, but also create a climate of fear and mistrust that affects society as a whole.

Incest and pedophilia are particularly disturbing and perverse because they occur within the family unit, where trust is expected and cherished. Incest often involves an abuse of power that destroys family relationships and leaves victims with profound psychological wounds.

Pedophilia, which involves the sexual exploitation of children, is especially harmful because children are unable to consent and are more vulnerable to abuse. Research has found that individuals with pedophilic tendencies often show abnormal brain structures and that their actions result in severe, long-lasting harm to their victims. (Cantor et al. 2008) These issues must be addressed with strong legal actions (castration?), robust support systems for survivors, and societal commitment to protecting the most vulnerable members of our community.

Rape: Definition, Causes, Consequences, Prevention

Rape (noun):
1: unlawful sexual activity and, usually, sexual intercourse carried out forcibly or under threat of injury, against a person's will or with a person who is beneath a certain age or incapable of valid consent because of mental illness, mental deficiency, intoxication, unconsciousness, or deception; compare sexual assault, statutory rape
2: an outrageous violation
3: an act or instance of robbing or despoiling or carrying away a person by force

Rape is a violent crime involving nonconsensual sexual intercourse or penetration, typically carried out through force, coercion, or when the victim is unable to give consent. It is a severe violation of a person's autonomy and dignity, with lasting physical, emotional, and psychological effects.

There are many causes of rape, often rooted in power dynamics, societal norms, and personal motivations. Some perpetrators commit rape to exert dominance and control, while others act due to deep-seated misogyny (prejudice against women), entitlement, or lack of empathy. Alcohol and drug use can also play a role, impairing judgment and reducing a person's ability to resist or give informed consent.

Cultural factors, such as victim-blaming, inadequate sex education, and toxic masculinity can contribute to the normalization of sexual violence. Toxic masculinity refers to harmful behaviors and beliefs about what it means to be a man. These include the ideas that men must only be tough, aggressive, and unemotional. Such beliefs can lead to negative outcomes, like promoting violence, suppressing emotions, and devaluing women.

The consequences of rape are devastating. Victims often suffer from post-traumatic stress disorder (PTSD), depression, anxiety, and suicidal thoughts. Many victims experience physical injuries, sexually transmitted infections, and *unplanned pregnancies.* Socially, rape survivors may face stigma, shame, and difficulties in relationships, education, and employment. The legal system can also add to their trauma, as reporting and seeking justice is often an emotionally exhausting process.

Statistics highlight the alarming prevalence of rape. According to the World Health Organization (2013), about one in three women worldwide experiences physical or sexual violence in her lifetime, with rape being one of the most severe forms. In the U.S., the Rape, Abuse & Incest National Network (RAINN) reports that every 68 seconds, an American is sexually assaulted, and only 25 out of every 1,000 rapists are convicted. (2025) Men and children are also victims, with about one in 33 men experiencing rape in his lifetime.

Preventing rape requires a collective effort, including education on consent, stricter legal consequences for perpetrators, better support for survivors, and shifting cultural attitudes toward gender equality and respect. Ending rape is not just about punishing criminals but changing the mindset that allows sexual violence to persist in society.

Resources

RAINN is the nation's largest anti-sexual-violence organization. RAINN created and operates the National Sexual Assault Hotline in partnership with more than 1,000 local sexual assault service providers across the country. If you or someone you know has been sexually assaulted, help is available.

- Chat online at online.rainn.org.
- Call someone who can help: (800) 656-HOPE (4673)

Eliminate Incest

Incest: Definition, Causes, Consequences, and Prevention

incest (noun):
sexual intercourse between persons so closely related that they are forbidden by law to marry

Incest is sexual activity between family members who are too closely related to marry legally. This includes relationships between parents and children, siblings, or other close relatives. It is widely condemned in most cultures and is illegal in many countries because of the harm it causes to victims and families.

There are many causes of incest, often linked to power imbalances, secrecy, and family dysfunction. In some cases, an abuser takes advantage of their authority over a younger or weaker family member. Substance abuse, mental illness, and a history of family violence can increase the risk. In homes where boundaries are weak or where children are neglected, the chances of incest occurring may be higher. Additionally, generational cycles of abuse can play a role, where victims of incest may become abusers themselves if they do not receive proper help.

The consequences of incest are severe and long-lasting. Victims often suffer from deep emotional and psychological trauma, including depression, anxiety, low self-esteem, and post-traumatic stress disorder (PTSD). Many people struggle with trust and relationships, making it difficult to form healthy connections later in life. Physically, incest can result in *unplanned pregnancies* and a higher risk of genetic disorders in children born from incestuous relationships. Victims may also experience self-harm, suicidal thoughts, or substance abuse as ways to cope with their trauma. (RAINN 2025)

Statistics show that incest is more common than many people realize. According to studies, about one in five girls and one in thirteen boys experience sexual abuse, and the National Center for PTSD reports that about 30% of child sexual abuse cases are committed by family members (Whealin & Barnett 2025). Because incest often happens in secret, the true numbers may be even higher, as many victims never come forward due to fear, shame, or manipulation by their abusers.

Preventing incest requires strong family boundaries, education, and open communication. Teaching children about body safety, consent, and how to recognize inappropriate behavior is crucial. Parents and caregivers should create safe environments where children feel comfortable reporting any abuse. Schools and communities must provide awareness programs to help spot and stop abuse early. Stricter laws and stronger punishments for offenders also play a role in reducing incest. Counseling and support services for survivors can help break the cycle of abuse, ensuring that victims receive the help they need to heal.

Incest is a serious issue with devastating effects, but with education, awareness, and strong legal action, it can be prevented. Protecting children and ensuring safe family environments must be a priority for society.

Eliminate Pedophilia

Pedophilia: Definition, Causes, Consequences, and Prevention

Pedophilia (noun):
sexual perversion in which children are the preferred sexual object

Pedophilia is a psychiatric disorder in which an adult or older adolescent experiences persistent sexual attraction to prepubescent children, typically under the age of 13. It is classified as a mental disorder in the *Diagnostic and Statistical Manual of Mental Disorders (DSM-5)*. (American Psychiatric Association 2013) However, not all pedophiles act on their urges—some recognize their condition and seek help to prevent harming children.

The exact causes of pedophilia are not fully understood, but research suggests a combination of biological, psychological, and environmental factors. Brain scan studies have shown differences in the brains of pedophiles, particularly in areas related to impulse control and sexual behavior. Childhood trauma, such as sexual abuse or neglect, may also contribute to the development of pedophilic tendencies. Some researchers believe abnormal hormone levels or genetic predispositions play a role. Additionally, early exposure to sexual content, including pornography or inappropriate sexual experiences, may influence sexual preferences later in life.

Pedophilia has devastating effects on victims, society, and even the individuals who struggle with the disorder. Children who experience sexual abuse often suffer long-term emotional and psychological damage, including depression, anxiety, PTSD, and trust issues. STIs and *unplanned pregnancies* may result. Studies show that child sexual abuse survivors are at higher risk for substance abuse, self-harm, and suicidal thoughts.

Beyond individual victims, pedophilia fuels criminal activities such as child pornography and human trafficking, increasing the burden on mental health and law enforcement systems. Those who act on their urges face legal consequences, including imprisonment and mandatory registration as sex offenders. Even those who seek help before committing a crime may struggle with social stigma and isolation.

Preventing child sexual abuse requires a multilevel approach involving individuals, families, and communities. Education and awareness programs can help children understand bodily safety, boundaries, and warning signs of abuse. Parents should monitor online activities and interactions, as many predators use the internet to target children. Providing therapy and support for individuals who recognize their urges but do not want to act on them can prevent harm, with treatments including CBT and medications that reduce sexual impulses. Governments must also continue enforcing strict penalties for child sexual abuse and child pornography while investing in technology to track and stop online predators.

Statistics highlight the seriousness of this issue. The *National Center for Missing & Exploited Children* reported that online child exploitation cases increased by 97% from 2019 to 2021. The WHO estimates that one in five women and one in seven men worldwide experienced sexual abuse as children (O'Donnell 2021).

Pedophilia is a complex issue with devastating consequences for victims and society. While its causes remain unclear, prevention should focus on education, mental health support, strict law enforcement, and online safety measures. Protecting children from sexual abuse must be a top priority for individuals, families, and governments worldwide.

Our goal is to reduce unplanned pregnancies to reduce stress on women and reduce abortions. We can do this together!

Chapter 18

Eliminate Sex Trafficking

Sex trafficking is a severe issue affecting individuals of all ages, leading to profound personal and societal consequences. Recent data from the U.S. Department of State's 2023 *Trafficking in Persons Report* highlights that numerous governments worldwide have documented patterns of human trafficking, including forced labor and sexual slavery (Novotney 2023).

In the United States, the Bureau of Justice Statistics reported that between January 2008 and June 2010, sex-trafficking victims were predominantly white (26%) or Black (40%). Furthermore, a national survey released in January 2023 indicated that 62% of 457 survivors had been cited, arrested, or detained by law enforcement at least once, and among those, 71% had or have criminal records due to actions taken while being trafficked. (Banks & Kyckelhahn 2011)

The health impacts on sex-trafficking victims are profound and multifaceted. Seven in ten human-trafficking victims are women and girls. According to the American Psychological Association, trafficking can lead to severe mental health issues, including anxiety disorders, PTSD, depression, and substance abuse. Additionally, victims often suffer from physical health problems such as sexually transmitted infections, *unplanned pregnancies*, and injuries resulting from abuse. (Novotney 2023)

The involvement of victims in pornography, prostitution, and online sex work exacerbates these health issues and contributes to the perpetuation of trauma. Exposure to repeated exploitation can lead to long-term psychological distress and hinder recovery efforts.

The societal implications of sex trafficking are extensive. Communities bear the economic burden of providing health care, legal services, and rehabilitation for survivors. Moreover, the sexualization of minors and the normalization of exploitative behaviors perpetuate cycles of abuse and exploitation.

Addressing the sex-trafficking crisis requires a comprehensive approach, including prevention, protection, prosecution, and partnership. Enhancing public awareness, providing support services for survivors, and implementing stringent legal measures against perpetrators are critical steps toward mitigating this pervasive issue.

Eliminate Prostitution and Online Sex Work

Prostitution and Online Sex Work: Causes, Consequences, and Statistics

Prostitution (noun):
1: the act or practice of engaging in sex acts, especially sexual intercourse, in exchange for pay: sex work
2: the state of being involved in or devoted to corrupt or unworthy purposes

Prostitution is the exchange of sex for money, goods, or services. In recent years, online platforms like OnlyFans have changed how sex work is done, allowing individuals to sell explicit content directly to customers. While some argue that these platforms provide a safer alternative to street prostitution, both forms of sex work have serious consequences for individuals and society.

There are many reasons why people enter prostitution or online sex work. Sexual trafficking, coercion, poverty, lack of job opportunities, and financial desperation often push women and men into selling their bodies. Many come from abusive backgrounds or have experienced sexual exploitation at a young age. Drug addiction is another common factor, with some individuals using sex work to support their habits. The rise of OnlyFans and similar sites has also made it easier for young people to be lured into the sex industry, with the promise of fast money and financial independence. However, many later find themselves trapped, unable to leave due to dependency on the income or fear of public shame.

The consequences of prostitution and online sex work are severe. For women, engaging in sex work—whether in person or online—can lead to physical danger, exploitation, and long-term psychological harm. Studies show that many prostitutes experience high rates of violence, sexual assault, and PTSD. Even online, women face harassment, stalking, and threats, as well as the risk of their explicit content being leaked and used against them. Many who enter sex work hoping for financial freedom find later that the emotional toll and social stigma leave them feeling isolated and trapped.

Prostitution increases the risk of *unplanned pregnancies* and STI's due to unprotected sex, exploitation, and lack of reproductive health care. Unplanned pregnancies can trap women in poverty, force them into difficult choices, or put children at risk of unstable living conditions. Studies show that many women in prostitution experience high rates of sexual violence, making pregnancy prevention even harder. Providing education, health care access, and exit programs can help reduce unplanned pregnancies and support women in leaving the cycle of exploitation.

Men are also negatively affected. Regular consumption of paid sexual content can create unrealistic expectations about relationships and intimacy. Many men who subscribe to OnlyFans or hire prostitutes develop an unhealthy view of women, seeing them as objects rather than equals. Studies show that frequent porn or sex work consumption can reduce life satisfaction, increase loneliness, and make it harder to form genuine relationships. Some men become financially ruined, spending thousands of dollars on subscriptions or escorts while neglecting their real lives.

Society as a whole suffers from the normalization of prostitution and online sex work. The growing acceptance of OnlyFans-style platforms contributes to the exploitation of young women, who may be pressured into selling explicit content without fully understanding the long-term consequences. Additionally, prostitution remains linked to human trafficking, in which vulnerable individuals—often minors—are forced into the sex trade against their will. Studies show that countries where prostitution is legalized often see an increase in trafficking and organized crime rather than a decrease in exploitation.

Statistics highlight the growth of the industry. OnlyFans has millions of content creators, with many earning little despite promises of wealth. The global sex industry is worth over $180 billion, with online platforms rapidly expanding. Many women who join OnlyFans later regret it, finding that their content remains online forever, affecting future job prospects and personal relationships.

To combat the harms of prostitution and online sex work, society must address the root causes, such as poverty, lack of education, and exploitation.

Stricter regulations, better support for those trying to leave the industry, and education on healthy relationships can help protect individuals from the damaging effects of the sex trade.

Resources
• Human Trafficking Hotline: 1-888-373-7888
https://humantraffickinghotline.org/en
https://www.dhs.gov/blue-campaign/report-human-trafficking

Eliminate Pornography

Pornography: Definition, Negative Consequences, and Growth

Pornography (noun):
1:   the depiction of erotic behavior (as in pictures or writing) intended to cause sexual excitement
2:   material (such as books or photographs) that depicts erotic behavior and is intended to cause sexual excitement
3:   the depiction of acts in a sensational manner so as to arouse a quick, intense emotional reaction

Pornography refers to sexually explicit material, including videos, images, and literature, designed to sexually arouse viewers. It has become more accessible than ever due to the internet, with millions of websites offering free (though still monetized by clicks) and paid content. While some argue that pornography is a form of entertainment, studies suggest it has serious negative effects on individuals and society. Think about it. People are getting off watching other people have sex? Really? We're better than this!

For men, excessive pornography use can lead to addiction, unrealistic expectations about sex, and difficulties in relationships. Studies show that frequent porn consumption can rewire the brain, reducing sensitivity to real-life intimacy and increasing the need for more extreme content to feel aroused. Many men who watch pornography regularly struggle with erectile dysfunction, lower self-esteem, and difficulty forming deep emotional connections. Research also suggests that heavy porn use can lead to a lack of motivation and reduced interest in real-life romantic relationships.

Five signs of porn induced erectile dysfunction (PIED):
1. Difficulty getting an erection
2. Difficulty maintaining an erection during sex
3. Ease in getting erection to porn, but not to imagination or real sex
4. Greater excitement for porn than real sexual experiences
5. No arousal during real sexual experiences

According to Robert Weiss, PhD (2021):

> For many healthy adolescent and adult males, an unexpected consequence of heavy porn use is sexual dysfunction. Most often, this manifests as erectile dysfunction (ED), but porn-using males also sometimes struggle with delayed ejaculation (DE) and anorgasmia (the inability to reach orgasm). Depending on the research, anywhere from 17% to 58% of men who self-identify as heavy/compulsive/addicted users of porn struggle with some form of sexual dysfunction. Basically, research tells us that the more porn one uses, the more likely sexual dysfunction is.

"Porn has poisoned the souls of men, making them predators of the very ones they are called to protect (women and children)."
~Andrew Whalen

Women are also negatively affected by pornography, both as viewers and as individuals affected by its influence on men. Many women report feeling pressured to meet unrealistic beauty and sexual-performance standards set by the porn industry. Pornography often portrays women as objects rather than as human beings, promoting harmful ideas about consent and respect. Studies show that exposure to pornography can increase the likelihood of aggression toward women and normalize violent or degrading behavior in sexual relationships.

> ...[T]he United States still has the highest rate of teen pregnancy among industrialized nations—nearly one million American women aged 15–19 become pregnant each year. A majority of these pregnancies are unplanned ... Previous RAND Corporation research established a link between such exposure and the onset of sexual activity among teens (see RB-9068). Extending this work, a team of RAND researchers examined the link between teen pregnancy and exposure to sexual content on TV. The study found that frequent exposure to TV sexual content was associated with a significantly greater likelihood of teen pregnancy in the following three years. (Chandra et al. 2008)

The effects of pornography extend beyond individuals, harming society as a whole. Research links widespread pornography consumption to increased rates of divorce, infidelity, and dissatisfaction in relationships. It also contributes to the demand for exploitative content, including child pornography and human trafficking. Many pornographic websites fail to verify the age or consent of performers, leading to widespread abuse and exploitation. Additionally, pornography can have a negative impact on young people, shaping their views on sex before they have the maturity to understand healthy relationships.

Statistics reveal the alarming growth of the pornography industry. Studies estimate that over 35% of all internet downloads are porn related. Popular porn sites receive more traffic than major platforms like Netflix, Amazon, and X (Formerly Twitter) combined. The global pornography industry is worth over $100 billion, and its influence continues to expand through new technology, including virtual reality and artificial intelligence. Surveys suggest that the average age of first exposure to pornography is around 11 years old, meaning many children are being exposed to explicit content before they even understand what healthy relationships look like.

Preventing the negative effects of pornography requires education, self-awareness, and responsible online behavior. Schools and parents should teach young people about the dangers of porn addiction and the importance of real, respectful relationships. Individuals struggling with excessive porn use can seek help through counseling or support groups. Society must also push for stronger regulations to prevent exploitation within the porn industry and protect vulnerable individuals from harm.

While pornography may seem harmless to some, its widespread impact on individuals, relationships, and culture is significant. Recognizing its dangers and making informed choices about media consumption can help create a healthier society.

"All the trafficking in the world is being funded through pornography," and "If you are watching pornography, you are either watching a crime scene or you are funding one."
~Troy Brewer

Resource
• Porn Addiction Help: https://www.addictionhelp.com/porn/resources/

Warning about Sexting

Sexting (noun):
the sending of sexually explicit messages or images by cell phone (and/or online)

Sexting and sending nude photos electronically can be very risky. Once you send a photo, you lose control over who sees it. This can lead to problems such as bullying, unplanned sharing, and damage to your reputation. In some cases, people may even use these images to blackmail you, a crime known as sexual extortion. When someone threatens to share your private photos unless you give them money or favors, it can cause a lot of stress and harm. Even if you think nude pics and videos are deleted, they're not. They leave a digital imprint where a skilled computer user can recover "deleted" photos and videos.

Research shows that many young people who engage in sexting later face serious consequences. For example, a national study found that youths who sent explicit images were more likely to experience sexual extortion and other negative outcomes. (Finkelhor et al. 2024) These risks, including meeting someone in person that you met online, can also lead to rape, kidnapping and being sexually trafficked, *unplanned pregnancies*, abuse, sexually transmitted diseases, and deep emotional trauma. It is important to think carefully before sending any intimate photos online, as the long-term effects can be very damaging to your personal life and well-being.

Clarifying Censorship

Censor (noun):
> 1: a person who supervises conduct and morals, such as:
> > a: an official who examines materials (such as publications or films) for objectionable material
> >
> > b: an official (as in a time of war) who reads communications (such as letters) and deletes material considered sensitive or harmful

The term "censorship" often carries a negative meaning in news and media because it's linked to suppressing differing opinions and spreading biased information. Some media outlets have been accused of leaving out viewpoints they don't agree with, leading to claims of unfair reporting and sharing only part of the truth. This kind of action can be seen as manipulative and goes against the principles of balanced journalism. This is bad censorship.

On the other hand, these same media outlets might criticize parents who limit what their children see in entertainment and education. They present themselves as defenders of free speech and label such parental controls as opposing this freedom. The debate over censorship is complex, with people holding different opinions about when and why it should be used. Some believe censorship is necessary to protect others from harmful or offensive content. Others argue that it limits freedom of speech and access to important information. Understanding the reasons behind censorship helps us see why it's such a complicated issue. In the case of these parents, they are seeking to protect their children, therefore, trying to conduct good censorship.

It's important to realize that just because something is legal doesn't mean it's good for individuals or society. For example, while pornography is protected under the First Amendment and is legal within certain limits, its availability, especially to minors, raises serious concerns about its effects on personal and societal well-being. Despite legal restrictions and parental controls, the widespread nature of the internet often allows children to encounter such material, highlighting the challenges in effectively regulating content.

In the end, everyone practices some form of censorship in their lives. The question is, are you exercising good or bad censorship in your own life? We all make choices about what we watch, read, and listen to, based on what we believe according to personal values and societal norms. Some people self-regulate more strictly about these choices while others are more relaxed. But in some way, we all supervise, or censor, our own actions and morals.

Good Censorship

As a mental health professional and life coach, I guide individuals to censor or intentionally filter aspects of their lives that hinder personal growth and well-being. To exercise good censorship, this process involves consciously choosing what to allow into one's life and what to exclude, fostering a healthier and more fulfilling existence.

One critical area of focus is dietary habits. By encouraging clients to eliminate or censor unhealthy foods and beverages, we support them in adopting nutritious alternatives that enhance physical health and energy levels. This conscious censoring of detrimental dietary choices leads to improved overall well-being and sets the foundation for a more vibrant lifestyle.

Managing, or censoring, social interactions is equally important. I help individuals identify and set boundaries with toxic relationships that drain energy and negatively affect mental health. Establishing these boundaries empowers clients to cultivate a supportive social environment, essential for personal growth and emotional stability. Creating boundaries with negative individuals allows one to maintain control and focus on positive influences.

Time management is another vital aspect of censoring oneself. I assist clients in evaluating their daily activities to identify and reduce time spent on unproductive pursuits, such as excessive video gaming and smartphone overuse and addiction. Redirecting this time toward meaningful and goal-oriented activities enhance productivity and personal satisfaction. By consciously choosing, or censoring, how to allocate time, individuals can make significant strides toward achieving their objectives.

Furthermore, I guide clients in curating—censoring—the media they consume. Encouraging the selection of uplifting and positive content over material that is violent, degrading, has foul language, or is harmful, contributes to better mental health. This intentional filtering fosters a more optimistic mindset and reduces exposure to negative influences that can impede personal development. Recognizing and overcoming negative influences by censoring is crucial for shaping a positive mindset and overall well-being. This is what good parenting involves.

By implementing these strategies, individuals can effectively censor aspects of their lives (and their children's) that do not align with their values and goals. This proactive approach leads to enhanced mental and physical health, increased productivity, and a more positive and fulfilling life journey. I talk about censorship in light of discussing porn and other negative activities, they need censored.

Okay, sorry, I digressed for a moment and slipped into counseling/coaching mode. Back to the task at hand.

Our goal is to reduce unplanned pregnancies to reduce stress on women and reduce abortions. We can do this together!

Excerpt from Prince's Interview on Censorship in His Later Days (unknown source):
"I had a discussion with a friend of mine recently, and I asked him if he thought that a very popular horror film that he watched, if it was real or fake, and he said it's fake. I said, 'Why don't you tell me one of the scenes from it?' and he said, 'Okay,' and he told me one of the scenes. I said, 'It's with you, isn't it? And it's gonna be with you the rest of your life, isn't it?' And he said, 'What do you mean?' I said, 'It's now a part of you. It's now part of your fiber. What you watch and what you listen to turns into you, and I think it's important that we start to have some sort of censorship. We've turned that word into a bad word, but we're really jacking our kids' brains up, you know, we need to start to examine the stuff (we and our kids watch and listen to) a little more closely. Turn the TV off, for just like a week. What if we just shut down for a week and everybody had to find stuff to do?'"

Chapter 19

Eliminate Alcohol/Drug Use, Overuse, and Abuse

Alcohol and Drug Use: Causes, Consequences, and Impact on Society

Alcohol and drug use range from casual or recreational consumption to full-blown addiction. Casual use refers to occasional drinking or drug use in social settings, while addiction is a chronic disease in which a person loses control over their substance use, leading to dependence. While some believe casual use is harmless, both alcohol and drug consumption can have serious consequences, not just for the user but also for society as a whole.

There are many causes of substance use and addiction. Some people start using alcohol or drugs out of curiosity, peer pressure, or to cope with stress, trauma, or mental health issues like depression and anxiety. Others may have family histories of addiction, making them more vulnerable to dependency. Environmental factors, such as growing up in a household where substance abuse is common, also increase the risk. Easy access to alcohol and drugs, as well as media and cultural influences that glamorize substance use, contribute to its widespread acceptance. Over time, what starts as occasional use can turn into addiction as the brain becomes dependent on the substance to function normally.

The consequences of alcohol and drug use are severe for both men and women. Physically, long-term substance abuse can cause liver disease, heart problems, brain damage, weakened immune systems, and overdoses, which can be fatal. Addiction also affects mental health, leading to increased rates of depression, anxiety, paranoia, and suicidal thoughts. Many addicts experience financial problems, job loss, and homelessness due to their inability to function in daily life.

Substance abuse has a significant impact on relationships and sexual behavior. Alcohol and drugs lower inhibitions, leading to risky sexual activity, including unprotected sex, multiple partners, and an increased risk of STIs. **Studies show that substance use is a major factor in unplanned pregnancies, with one study showing alcohol being involved in 57% (about 6 out of 10) of unplanned pregnancies.** (Shafique et al. 2022) Women under the influence may also be more vulnerable to sexual assault, as intoxication impairs judgment and the ability to give clear consent.

There's a great debate going on: Is intoxicated sex consensual sex? It's a fine line between a girl being tipsy and still having full control of her faculties to give consent versus being impaired or incapacitated to the point of not being able to give coherent consent. Guys, err on the side of caution and get it in your head that drunk sex **is not** consensual sex and you may save yourself from a lot of troubles down the road. You may also gain respect from the female you're with for respecting her and not taking advantage of her, regardless of whether she really wanted it or not.

Violence and crime are closely linked to alcohol and drug use. According to the National Institute on Alcohol Abuse and Alcoholism (NIAAA), alcohol is involved in about 40% of violent crimes, including assaults, domestic violence, and homicides. (2016) *Drug and Alcohol Review* (Abbey 2011) reports that nearly 30-75% of all sexual assaults involve alcohol consumption by the perpetrator, victim, or both. Drug use also fuels criminal activity, as addicts often engage in theft, prostitution, or drug dealing to support their habits. The opioid crisis, for example, has led to a dramatic rise in drug-related crimes and overdoses across the U.S.

Substance abuse also puts a huge strain on society. The CDC estimates that excessive alcohol use costs the U.S. over $250 billion annually due to health care expenses, lost productivity, law enforcement, and car accidents. (2024) Driving under the influence is a leading cause of fatal crashes, with alcohol being responsible for nearly 30% of all traffic-related deaths. Communities with high rates of substance abuse often struggle with increased homelessness, poverty, and broken families.

Celebrities who don't drink alcohol and/or don't use drugs (Savin et al. 2025), (Singh 2025)
Actress/singer Zendaya
Actress Anne Hathaway
Actor Tom Holland
Actress/singer Miley Cyrus
Actor/singer Zac Efron
Actor Robert Downey Jr.
Actor Rob Lowe
Actress Drew Barrymore
Actor Brad Pitt
Actor Ben Affleck
Actor Russell Brand
Singer Keith Urban
Singer John Mayer
Singer Elton John
Rapper Flavor Flav

Model Elle MacPherson

Actress/singer Demi Lovato

Model Tyra Banks

Rapper/producer Tyler the Creator

Rapper Pharrell Williams

Actress Natalie Portman

Rapper Nicki Minaj

Rapper Eminem

Singer Jessica Simpson

Actor Daniel Radcliffe

Actor Bradley Cooper

Actress/singer Jennifer Hudson

Actress Jamie Lee Curtis

Actor Anthony Hopkins

… and many more.

As a school psychologist, I am deeply concerned about the effects of prenatal exposure to alcohol and drugs on children's development. Fetal Drug and Fetal Alcohol Spectrum Disorders (FASD) encompass a range of physical, behavioral, and cognitive impairments resulting from alcohol exposure during pregnancy. These impairments can manifest at any time during childhood and often last a lifetime.

Some women may have abortions because of fetal birth defects—women should be reminded that their personal choices may cause birth defects and maybe they will want to prevent that possibility from ever happening by avoiding drugs and alcohol in general, especially if sexually active. The average person doesn't think about this, but those of us in education and mental health deal with Fetal Drug- and Fetal Alcohol-affected individuals on a daily basis.

Children with FASD may exhibit learning difficulties, attention deficits, and social challenges. Despite appearing physically typical and possessing average intelligence, they often struggle with impulse control, memory, and understanding consequences, leading to academic and behavioral issues in school settings.

It's possible that a mother may not have a serious or long-lasting problem after using drugs. But the same is not always true for a fetus. Drug-using mothers often give birth to drug babies. These children have a host of developmental problems. Prenatal drug exposure can result in neurodevelopmental disorders, affecting a child's emotional regulation and increasing the risk of mental health issues. These children may face difficulties in forming relationships and adapting to structured environments, further impacting their educational experiences.

Sometimes women are using, overusing, or abusing alcohol and other drugs, but they don't even know they're pregnant. This is why it's so important that any woman who is sexually active should have it in the back of her mind that not only is this behavior not good for her, but if she gets pregnant, it may be detrimental for her baby.

Early identification and intervention are crucial. By collaborating with educators, parents, and health care providers, school psychologists and special education teams can develop individualized support plans to address these children's unique needs, promoting better outcomes academically, socially, mentally, and emotionally.

Preventing addiction requires education, early intervention, and strong support systems. Schools and parents should teach young people about the dangers of substance abuse, while mental health services should be accessible to help those struggling with addiction. Stricter regulations on alcohol and drug distribution, as well as better rehabilitation programs, can help reduce the impact of substance abuse on individuals and society.

While casual alcohol and drug use may seem harmless, the risks of addiction and its devastating consequences are too great to ignore. Awareness, prevention, emphasis on morality and spirituality, and strong community efforts are key to tackling this ongoing crisis.

Our goal is to reduce unplanned pregnancies to reduce stress on women and reduce abortions. We can do this together!

"There's not a drug on earth that can make life meaningful."
~Sarah Kane

"Sobriety was not just about drugs and alcohol. I had to detox from anger, fear, resentment, and hate."
~Excerpt from post on The Thrive Project group page on Facebook

"If you need booze or drugs to enjoy your life to the fullest, then you're doing it wrong."
~Robin Williams

Part 4

Personal and Social Responsibility

Chapter 20

Message for Men:
Step Up to Responsibility

Men, we can do better. If you're having sex, you need to do everything you can to prevent an unplanned pregnancy and if you get a woman pregnant you need to man-up and be a responsible, positive support to that woman in her time of need. If you're not ready to try to prevent unplanned pregnancies or deal with getting a woman pregnant, or deal with the possibility of being a father, then you're not ready to be having sex. It's your responsibility as much as hers.

Being a responsible man is about more than just providing for yourself—it's about making a positive impact on your family, workplace, and community. Men have an important role as husbands, fathers, employees, and citizens, and taking that responsibility seriously benefits everyone around you. A strong work ethic, education, faith, and respect for women are key qualities that define responsible manhood. These qualities not only improve individual success, but also strengthen families and society as a whole. Every single person is a role model; the question is, are you a good role model or a bad role model? We are the role models, children are the mirrors, they mirror what they see us do.

Fatherhood: One of the most important responsibilities of a man is being a good father. Studies show that children raised in fatherless homes are more likely to struggle in life. According to the U.S. Census Bureau, about 18.3 million children in America—1 in 4—live without a biological, step, or adoptive father in the home. (Brewer 2023) Research from the National Fatherhood Initiative reveals that children in father-absent homes are four times more likely to live in poverty, more likely to engage in criminal behavior, and more likely to drop out of school. (Byers 2021) On the other hand, children with involved fathers perform better academically, have higher self-esteem, and are less likely to engage in risky behaviors. A two-parent home, in general, provides stability, discipline, and love, helping children grow into responsible adults.

Husband: Being a good husband is just as important as being a good father. A strong marriage sets the foundation for a stable home. Studies show that two-parent households provide better financial security and emotional support for children. The Institute for Family Studies found that children raised by married parents are more likely to graduate from high school, *avoid teen pregnancy*, and have successful careers. (Zill & Wilcox 2018) Marriage is not just about companionship; it's about teamwork, respect, and commitment. Treating a spouse with kindness, respect, and faithfulness creates a home environment where children learn how to build healthy relationships in the future.

Work Ethic and Education: A strong work ethic and education are also critical for a man's success. Hard work and dedication lead to financial stability and personal fulfillment. According to the U.S. Bureau of Labor Statistics, individuals with high school diplomas earn about $8,000 more per year than those without one, and those with a college degree earn nearly double. (2023) Education opens doors to better job opportunities and career growth, reducing the chance of financial struggles. Men who are committed to their work not only provide for their families, but also set examples for their children to follow.

Faith and Values: Religious faith is another important factor in responsible manhood. Studies show that men who actively practice their faith are more involved in their families, less likely to engage in substance abuse, and more likely to contribute positively to their communities. Faith teaches values such as honesty, kindness, and self-discipline. A 2019 study from Pew Research Center found that people who attend religious services regularly report higher levels of happiness and life satisfaction. Faith provides guidance, helping men navigate challenges and make moral decisions that benefit themselves and others.

Respect for Women: Respecting women is another key aspect of being a responsible man. Women should be treated with the same respect and dignity that men would want for their mothers, grandmothers, sisters, and daughters. This means being kind, listening, and supporting women in their goals and careers. Research from the World Health Organization (2025) shows that societies where women are treated equally experience lower crime rates, stronger economies, and healthier families. A real man does not degrade or mistreat women but instead uplifts and protects them. Be a protector, not a user and abuser.

Be a Role Model: Being a positive role model is essential in shaping future generations. Children learn by example, and when they see their fathers working hard, treating others with respect, and staying committed to their families, they are more likely to follow the same path. Strong male role models help boys grow into responsible men and teach girls what to expect from respectful and loving men. Surround yourself with male role models who strengthen, encourage, and guide you to be the best person you can be—men who will motivate you, not bring you down.

An example of a man role modeling to other men how to be positive role models to their children is Otto Kelly, former football running back turned pastor, Gang Specialist, Outreach Coordinator, Crisis Pregnancy Center Director, Chaplain for law enforcement, and leader in community services. Otto developed the "Dad-E Academy" to help young men step up as fathers growing in leadership, purpose, and resilience to combat fatherlessness. He also wrote the Sons to Men Curriculum covering key topics like "manhood, communication, fatherhood, and personal growth, this curriculum is designed to equip men for real change." (Sons to Men 2025)

In the end, responsible manhood is about making choices that benefit not just oneself but also one's family, community, and society. It requires hard work, faith, respect, and dedication. Men who embrace their roles as responsible citizens, husbands, fathers, and employees create better futures for themselves and those around them. By leading with integrity and setting a positive example, they help build stronger families, safer communities, and a more successful society.

Our goal is to reduce unplanned pregnancies to reduce stress on women and reduce abortions. We can do this together!

"The most important thing a father can do for his children is to love their mother."
~Theodore Hesburgh

"A man should never neglect his family for business."
~Walt Disney

"The greatest mark of a father is how he treats his children when no one is looking."
~Daniel Pearce

"The measure of a man is how he treats the women in his family."
~J.D. Vance

"Waste no more time arguing what a good man should be. Be one."
~Marcus Aurelius

"Any man can be a father, but it takes someone special to be a dad."
~Anne Geddes

Chapter 21

Message for Women: Make Choices to Thrive

Women play a vital role in shaping families, communities, and society. Being a responsible woman means making wise choices as a citizen, wife, mother, and employee. Education, a strong work ethic, faith, and self-respect are essential for personal success and the well-being of future generations. Women must take responsibility for their own lives by building their own strength and independence, including their sexuality, and not allow themselves to be manipulated or defined by what men say.

If you're easily swayed into bed by a smooth talker, then maybe you need to learn better boundaries and rethink the kind of man you want to hang with. Do you want to hang with a selfish man who will leave you stranded or coerce you into doing something you don't want to do, or do you want to be with a responsible man who will man-up and be by your side in your time of need? A stable two-parent home provides the best foundation for children, and women have a significant influence in creating and maintaining that stability.

Motherhood: One of the most important responsibilities of a woman is being a good mother. Being a positive role model is another important part of being a responsible woman. Whether as a mother, teacher, mentor, or leader in the workplace, women influence those around them. Children, especially daughters, look up to their mothers for guidance on how to navigate life. A mother who is responsible, hardworking, and respectful teaches her children to develop those same qualities. Sons who see their mothers demand respect and self-worth are more likely to treat women well in their own relationships.

Wife: Being a good wife is just as important as being a good mother. Respecting men is just as important as expecting respect from them. Healthy relationships are built on mutual respect and understanding, not on control or manipulation. Women who demand respect must also give it in return, treating their husbands, fathers, and brothers with kindness and appreciation. Studies show that strong marriages lead to happier, more successful families. Research from the Institute for Family Studies indicates that children raised in two-parent homes perform better academically, have lower rates of delinquency, *avoid teen pregnancies*, and are more likely to have stable relationships as adults. (Wilcox 2019) Women have a responsibility to help create these strong family units by choosing partners wisely, being faithful, and working through challenges and not giving up too easily.

Work Ethic and Education: Education and a strong work ethic are key to a woman's independence and future success. Studies show that women with higher education levels earn more money, have greater career opportunities, and are less likely to experience poverty. According to the National Center for Education Statistics, women now make up the majority of college graduates, and those with degrees earn, on average, $20,000 more per year than those without degrees. (2024) Financial independence allows women to provide for themselves and their children without having to depend on others for survival (if your significant other is out of the picture, which happens more often than it should). A strong work ethic ensures that they can achieve their goals, whether in a career or managing a household, and set a positive example for the next generation.

Faith and Values: Religious faith also plays an important role in guiding women's decisions and shaping their characters. Faith teaches values such as patience, kindness, self-respect, and perseverance. A study from the Pew Research Center found that women who regularly attend religious services report higher levels of life satisfaction and emotional well-being. (2019) Faith provides a moral foundation that helps women make choices that lead to stable, fulfilling lives. It also offers a sense of community and support during difficult times, which is essential for personal growth and family stability.

Responsibility and Choices: Women must also take responsibility for their own bodies and sexuality. Society often pressures women to seek validation from men, but self-worth should never be determined by what men think or say. No woman should allow herself to be coerced, manipulated, or deceived into making choices that are not in her best interest. It is up to each woman to protect herself from *unplanned pregnancies* and sexually transmitted infections. According to the Guttmacher Institute, nearly half of all pregnancies in the U.S. are unintended, and many of these could have been prevented with proper education and contraception. (2019) While both men and women are responsible for preventing pregnancy, women must ultimately take control of their own health and choices, ensuring they are not left in difficult situations because of someone else's decisions or irresponsibility.

Ultimately, women must strive for strength and wisdom in all areas of life. They must not allow themselves to be defined by society's expectations, smooth talkers, or unhealthy relationships. Instead, they should build their own futures through education, faith, and hard work while also fostering strong families and communities. A woman who respects herself, values her body, and takes responsibility for her choices is empowered to live a successful and meaningful life. By doing so, she not only betters her own life but also creates a legacy of strength, stability, and love for future generations.

Our goal is to reduce unplanned pregnancies to reduce stress on women and reduce abortions. We can do this together!

"A woman who is okay being alone is a powerful woman."
~unknown

"I remember my mother's prayers and they have always followed me. They have clung to me all my life."
~Abraham Lincoln

"A mother is she who can take the place of all others, but whose place no one else can take."
~Cardinal Meymillod

"My ultimate joy and happiness is being a wife and mother."
~Melissa Etheridge

"Mother's love transforms our house into a home, filled with warmth and laughter."
~unknown

"A man calling you baby means nothing. A man moving into your house means nothing. A man calling you his woman means nothing. A man giving you a baby means nothing. Let me make this even clearer, I'm about to hurt some feelings with this next one. A man marrying you means nothing. Do you know why? Because titles, gestures and words can be empty. They might look good on the surface, but they don't hold the weight of true commitment. True love and partnership aren't about what a man says, or the show he puts on. You know what means something? A man changing himself, his habits, his mindset, his priorities to keep you. A man who grows for you, who becomes better not just for you, *but because of you.* A man who values you so deeply that he's willing to let go of his old ways and put in the work to build a future where you both thrive.

That's what means something, actions speak louder than titles, growth speaks louder than promises, a man who truly cares just doesn't talk about it, he lives it. Pay attention to the man who shows you with his life, not just his lips. Real love isn't in the words he says, it's in the changes he makes to show he's all in."

~Unknown

(We can interchange "man" with "woman"; it goes both ways.)

Chapter 22

A Future of Hope and Understanding

Throughout this journey, we have explored the complex and deeply personal topic of abortion from various perspectives—legal, ethical, medical, and emotional. We have heard the voices of those who have faced unimaginable circumstances, those who have fought for life, and those who have made difficult choices. No matter where you stand in the debate, one truth remains: Every person's story matters.

As we move forward, let us shift from conflict to compassion, from division to dialogue. The abortion debate often feels like a battleground, but real change comes when we choose to listen, understand, and support one another.

Empathy Over Judgment

Imagine a world where we approach this issue not with anger or condemnation, but with a heart willing to hear and help. Instead of fighting, we can work together to ensure that every woman—regardless of her choice—feels supported, valued, and never alone. Whether it's expanding education on reproductive health, improving adoption resources, or providing emotional and financial support to women facing crisis pregnancies, there are tangible ways to create a culture that honors both life and choice with dignity.

Turning Pain into Purpose

Many of the most powerful stories in this book have come from those who have faced hardship, heartbreak, or regret—yet have turned their pain into purpose. Whether advocating for life, supporting women in need, or simply sharing their stories, they remind us that no life is without value, and no experience is without meaning.

If you have ever struggled with your past, your choices, or your beliefs, know this: Your story is not over. There is always hope. Healing is possible. And even in the most difficult circumstances, there is a path forward.

A Call to Action

As we close this book, I encourage you to take this conversation beyond these pages. Speak with kindness, listen with an open heart, and take action in ways that create a better future for all—whether through advocacy, education, or simply offering a helping hand.

No matter what has brought you here, my hope is that you leave with a deeper understanding of yourself, others, and the profound impact of the choices we make. Together, we can build a world where both life and love are cherished.

Because, at the end of the day, every life—born and unborn—has the potential to change the world.

Our goal is to reduce unplanned pregnancies to reduce stress on women and reduce abortions. We can do this together!

Chapter 23

Bonus Chapter

Practical Steps for Pro-Choice and Pro-Life Citizens, Organizations, and Politicians Uniting

Communities divided by abortion views share a common goal: fewer unintended pregnancies. Unintended pregnancy rates in the U.S. fell 15% between 2010 and 2019—from 42.1 to 35.7 per 1,000 women aged 15–44—yet they remain unacceptably high. (CDC 2023) Nearly 5% of women experienced unintended pregnancies in 2011; two-thirds carried to term and 17% ended in abortion. (Guttmacher Institute 2019) Worldwide, access to effective contraception has reduced unsafe abortions and prevented mother-to-child HIV transmission. However, 85% of women who stop using contraception become pregnant within a year. (World Health Organization 2019) Studies show that providing no-cost, highly effective birth control methods cuts both repeat abortions and teen births (Bearak et al. 2018), and free birth control programs reduce unplanned pregnancies and abortions substantially. (Duke-Ellis & Peipert 2012) Eliminating out-of-pocket costs also boosts consistent use of top-tier contraceptives, narrowing health disparities. (Mostafavi 2020)

1. Forge bipartisan consensus on sex education.

Both pro-choice and pro-life groups agree that accurate information prevents unintended pregnancies. The New York State Bipartisan Pro-Choice Legislative Caucus backs age-appropriate, medically accurate sex education that includes abstinence as an option. (2025) Republican lawmakers in Iowa and Indiana have introduced bills to require comprehensive sex ed in middle schools—despite historic abstinence-only policies. (Masserly 2023) Step one is expanding these bipartisan successes nationwide.

2. Expand access to no-cost contraception.

Cost remains a major barrier. States and insurers should cover all FDA-approved contraceptives with no out-of-pocket expense. Evidence shows no-cost programs and pharmacist-prescribed methods slash unplanned pregnancies and abortions. (Williams 2012) Federal and state budgets must prioritize these investments.

3. Strengthen support services for young parents.

Even with prevention, some pregnancies are unintended. Funding community health centers, parenting classes, and affordable childcare reduces stress on pregnant women and families—lowering the pressure that can lead to abortion.

4. Promote community-based outreach.

Local faith- and community-based organizations can bridge cultural gaps. Training volunteers—both pro-life and pro-choice—on contraception counseling, abstinence, and referral services harnesses shared values to support women in crisis.

5. Coordinate data and research.

Agencies like the CDC, Guttmacher Institute, and WHO should maintain transparent, shared data on unintended pregnancies and service outcomes. Joint task forces can analyze trends, spot gaps, and recommend policy tweaks.

6. Launch a unified public awareness campaign.

A national campaign featuring voices from both movements can destigmatize contraception and abstinence and highlight stories of prevention success. Messages emphasizing shared goals—healthier families, stronger communities—will resonate more broadly.

7. Enact supportive legislation.

Policymakers can cosponsor bills that combine funding for sex education, contraception access, and maternity support services. Crafting legislation with input from diverse stakeholders ensures durability across elections.

By taking these steps—grounded in strong evidence and united values—pro-choice and pro-life citizens, organizations, and politicians can dramatically reduce unintended pregnancies. That shared success will ease the burden on women and families, lower abortion rates, and strengthen our communities.

And Then There Were None (Abortionworker.com 2025)

And Then There Were None is a nonprofit organization founded and led by Abby Johnson to help abortion clinic workers leave the abortion industry. Abby worked for Planned Parenthood for eight years, working her way up through the ranks to become the clinic director of an abortion facility in Bryan, Texas. She was Planned Parenthood's Employee of the Year in 2008, but she walked away from her job in October 2009 after witnessing the abortion of a 13-week-old baby during an ultrasound-guided abortion.

She left Planned Parenthood and instantly became a national news headline for her defection. And Then There Were None is the only organization in the nation that helps abortion workers leave their jobs and find new careers outside of the abortion industry. Her bestselling book, *Unplanned*, was made into a feature film that debuted in theaters nationwide in March 2019 under the same name.

For over a decade, Johnson has been a leading voice to amplify the actual truth about abortion and the abortion industry. With over 700 healthcare workers who left the abortion industry and who have similar firsthand accounts to share, you can clearly see that Johnson's experience is not an isolated one. The issues to which they can attest regarding the abortion industry are systemic issues that deserve urgent attention and resolution.

Choosing a Family/Pregnancy Resource Center

Summary of article by Moira Gaul, MPH, Associate Scholar, Charlotte Lozier Institute (Gaul 2015):

Pregnancy Help Centers More Likely to be Welcomed into Neighborhoods Than Planned Parenthood

A 2014 Charlotte Lozier Institute poll found that communities prefer Pregnancy Help Centers (PHCs) over Planned Parenthood clinics. When asked if a Planned Parenthood was nearby, 58% said yes; among those without one, only 18% wanted one, while 19% did not. By contrast, just 39% reported having a PHC close by, but 42% said they would welcome one—and only 11% opposed—after learning PHCs provide free medical services and support without offering or referring for abortions.

Support for PHCs crosses political lines: 94% of self-identified pro-life and 87% of pro-choice respondents called them "very" or "fairly" necessary. Overall, 92% of women and 88% of men agreed these centers play an important role for women with unplanned pregnancies. Thousands of PHCs nationwide offer services such as ultrasounds, counseling, and parenting classes that improve maternal and child health. This widespread approval underscores the value Americans place on free, nonjudgmental pregnancy support programs.

____

<u>Be a More Informed Taxpayer Funding Planned Parenthood:</u>

<u>Hearing Wrap Up: Planned Parenthood Exposed: Examining the Horrific Abortion Practices at the Nation's Largest Abortion Provider</u>
United States Committee on the Judiciary, September 9, 2015
https://judiciary.house.gov/media/press-releases/hearing-wrap-up-planned-parenthood-exposed-examining-the-horrific-abortion

<u>VICTORY: Lawfare against Daleiden and Merritt, who exposed Planned Parenthood, is over</u>
Nancy Flanders, January 27, 2025
https://www.liveaction.org/news/victory-lawfare-daleiden-merritt-planned-parenthood-over/

<u>Viral Video: 'October Baby' Abortion Survivor Slams Planned Parenthood in Emotional Congressional Testimony</u>
Samuel Smith, Deputy Managing Editor, September 17, 2015
https://www.christianpost.com/news/viral-video-october-baby-abortion-survivor-slams-planned-parenthood-in-emotional-congressional-testimony.html

____

Dating

Dating can be a fun way to learn about yourself and others, but it also comes with challenges. By understanding the pros and cons and setting clear guidelines for appropriate ages, boundaries, and purposes, young people can have healthier, more positive experiences.

For most people, the goal of dating is to find a lifelong partner and build a supportive relationship. Since young adults are still exploring who they are—what psychologist Jeffrey Arnett calls "emerging adulthood," lasting roughly from ages 18 to 25—they often lack the self-understanding and emotional maturity needed for a true partnership. (Arnett 2000)

Brain research also shows that the prefrontal cortex, the part responsible for planning and impulse control, does not fully mature until around age 25. (Barlow 2014) Consequently, individuals under 25 may not be developmentally ready to shoulder the responsibilities and mutual support that healthy dating requires.

You rarely ever hear anyone say they waited too long to get married, but there are plenty of people who complain they married too young. Marrying later in life can strengthen a relationship. While about 45% of U.S. marriages end in divorce, that rate rises to around 60% for couples who marry between ages 20 and 25. (Divorce.com 2024) Young couples who do divorce most often cite money troubles, poor communication, lack of commitment, and emotional or physical abuse as the reasons their marriages failed.

Nevertheless, many choose to date earlier, so it's wise to follow these tips:
1. **Date with purpose.** Decide whether you're looking for friendship, companionship, or a serious commitment. Be honest with yourself and your partner about your intentions.
2. **Set clear boundaries.** Agree on emotional and physical limits before you begin dating. Respect each other's comfort levels, and communicate openly if boundaries need adjusting.
3. **Balance priorities.** Maintain hobbies, school, work, and family time. Healthy relationships grow best when both partners lead full, balanced lives.
4. **Practice self-awareness.** Check in with yourself about why you're dating. Ensure you're not seeking validation or using dating to fix personal issues.

By recognizing the natural process of self-development and following thoughtful guidelines, young people can enjoy healthier, more respectful dating experiences—even before they reach full adulthood, if they choose to do so, in spite of the statistics stacked against them. Here's some more food for thought.

The Pros of Dating

Dating helps people build social skills. It teaches communication, respect, and teamwork as you make plans, listen, and learn about another person's feelings. Dating can boost self-confidence by giving you chances to try new activities and explore shared interests. It also offers emotional support: Having someone who cares about you can make tough times easier.

The Cons of Dating

On the flip side, dating can bring stress and distraction. Balancing school, hobbies, and relationships isn't always easy, and grades or friendships may suffer if you're not careful. Emotional risks include heartbreak or peer pressure to move too fast. Young people might feel rushed into situations they aren't ready for, leading to regret or confusion.

Age Guidelines

- **Middle school to early high school (ages 12–15):** Focus on friendships and group outings rather than one-on-one dates.
- **Late high school (ages 16–18):** You can start casual, low-key dates like going to a movie or a sports event with a small group.
- **Post high school (ages 18–25):** One-on-one dates become more appropriate. At this age, you can explore deeper conversations and shared responsibilities.

Boundaries and Respect

Setting boundaries keeps everyone comfortable. Decide together what activities feel right—no one should feel pressured into physical contact they're not ready for. Use respectful language, avoid teasing or put-downs, and honor promises. Always ask for consent before hugs, kisses, or holding hands. If either person feels unsafe or uncomfortable, it's okay to pause or stop dating until both agree.

Purposes of Dating

- **Friendship:** Getting to know new people and forming supportive connections.
- **Learning:** Growing social and emotional skills like listening, compromise, and empathy.
- **Fun:** Enjoying shared hobbies, movies, or events in a trusting environment.
- **Commitment:** For older teens/young adults, dating can prepare you for serious, long-term relationships by teaching responsibility and loyalty.

Tips for Healthy Dating

1. **Communicate openly.** Share your thoughts and feelings honestly.
2. **Maintain balance.** Keep up with schoolwork, family time, and hobbies.
3. **Seek advice.** Talk with trusted adults—parents, teachers, or counselors—when you have questions or concerns.
4. **Be yourself.** Genuine relationships grow from authenticity, not trying to be someone else.

Dealing with a Breakup

Breakups hurt — a lot. They can leave you feeling empty, confused, and like your future suddenly changed. That pain comes from real loss: the person, the plans you made together, and the daily routines you shared. It's normal to ride an emotional roller coaster — sadness, anger, relief, guilt — sometimes all in one day. Healing takes time, and that's okay.

There are things you can do to feel better sooner. First, give yourself permission to grieve. Cry, journal, or talk about it. At the same time, set clear boundaries: limit contact with your ex and avoid stalking them online. Seeing their posts will only slow your recovery. Lean on friends and family for support — people want to help even if it feels scary to reach out. If things feel overwhelming, a counselor can give you tools to cope.

Take care of your body and mind. Sleep, eat well, move your body, and try calming practices like deep breathing or short meditations. Create healthy distractions: learn a new skill, pick up an old hobby, or plan small adventures. Rituals can help with closure — pack up reminders, write a letter you don't send, or visit a place that mattered and say goodbye in your own way. These actions make the ending real and help you move forward.

Finally, use this time to rebuild who you are. Reflect on what you learned, forgive yourself and the other person when you're ready, and avoid rushing into a new relationship to mask the pain. Practice kindness toward yourself; healing isn't a race. Over time, the sharp pain fades, you grow stronger, and you'll be ready for healthy relationships again. A breakup feels like the end at first — but with patience and care, it becomes the start of a new chapter. Know this – if you date, you will experience heartbreak at some point, so learn how to deal with it maturely.

By weighing the benefits and risks, knowing age-appropriate rules, and respecting boundaries, dating can be a safe and rewarding part of growing up.

Resources

• *The New Rules for Love, Sex, and Dating* book by Andy Stanley

• *He's Just Not That into You* self-improvement book written by Greg Behrendt and Liz Tuccillo (could be flipped for a guy as well, reader discretion is advised)

• *It's Called a Breakup Because It's Broken* book by Greg Behrendt and Amiira Ruotola-Behrendt (could be flipped for a guy as well, reader discretion is advised)

Modesty

Scene: Older man talking to a younger, minimally clothed woman, which leaves little to the imagination.

Man: "Hi darling, how much?"

Woman: "How much for what?"

Man: "You know, for a good time."

Woman: "What do you mean, you think I'm a prostitute?"

Man: "Well, aintcha?"

Woman: "Heck no!"

Man: "Well then why you advertising if you ain't selling?"

Modesty—for both women and men—means showing respect for yourself and others through how you dress, act, and speak, and it offers many benefits. When you choose clothing that isn't too flashy or risqué, you help others feel comfortable and focus on who you are, not what you wear or what you look like. Research shows that people who practice modest self-presentation often enjoy better social relationships and higher well-being. (Zheng & Wu 2019)

In behavior, modesty means listening more than talking and sharing credit when things go well. This builds trust and teamwork because people feel valued and respected. Modest individuals tend to have higher emotional intelligence, which helps them understand others' feelings and react kindly (Zheng & Wu 2019). This makes friendships stronger and reduces conflict.

A modest personality avoids bragging about achievements. Instead, modest people let their work speak for itself. Studies link trait modesty to healthier brain function in areas responsible for self-control and social thinking. (Qiu et al. 2017) This suggests that modesty supports both mental health and good decision-making.

Modesty of character means staying humble when praised and forgiving when wronged. Humble people are less likely to give in to peer pressure, care less about what people think and more about doing right, and are more likely to help others. They often report higher life satisfaction and lower stress. By focusing on values rather than appearance or status, they build deeper, more meaningful connections.

In all these areas—dress, behavior, personality, and character—modesty helps you feel better about yourself and improves your relationships. It also supports mental and social health by encouraging self-awareness, empathy, and respect for others. Embracing modesty can lead to a happier, more balanced life.

About The Author:

Wayne Van Der Wal grew up inside the beltway of Washington, DC, in Falls Church, Virginia (with time also spent in Michigan, Pennsylvania, Wyoming). He moved to the Reno/Lake Tahoe area of Nevada when he was 20. In recent years, he has split his time between Los Angeles and Reno/Lake Tahoe.

His professional work experience extends over three decades and includes being a school psychologist (Ed.S, NCSP), school counselor (MA), and past president of his state association, Nevada Association of School Psychologists (NVASP). He has a BA in social psychology. He added private practice life coaching in 2020 to help individuals live their best life ever when he semi-retired from working in public schools.

Wayne has worked in both public and private settings with clients of all ages, genders, sexual orientations, socioeconomic statuses, and diverse racial, religious, and ethnic backgrounds, as well as working with individuals with disabilities.

He also has over 30 years of experience in faith-based ministries serving children, youth, college students, singles, married couples, divorced individuals, inmates, and inner-city communities.

To Contact Wayne:

Visit WayneVanDerWal.com or TheGospelofSantaClaus.com.

Wayne's Other Books can be found online and in stores:
The Gospel of Santa Claus: Inspired by the True Story of Saint Nicholas
Beware! Corkie the Yorkie is a Sock Thief!
Embrace the Van Der Wal Effect! Helping you be More Productive at Work, School, and Life

Bibliographies

For all definitions:
Merriam-Webster. Merriam-Webster.com Dictionary. Accessed July 9, 2024. https://www.merriam-webster.com.

Chapter 6

Dobbs v. Jackson Women's Health Organization, 597 U.S. 215, 2022. https://www.supremecourt.gov/opinions/21pdf/19-1392_6j37.pdf.

Al-Samarrai, Riath. 2015. "Cristiano Ronaldo Unplanned Baby Wanted Abortion Reveals Star's Mum; New Film Gives Unique Look: Real Madrid Great Nearly Never Was." *Daily Mail*, April 4. https://www.dailymail.co.uk/sport/football/article-3304032/Cristiano-Ronaldo-unplanned-baby-wanted-abortion-reveals-star-s-mum-new-film-gives-unique-look-Real-Madrid-great-nearly-never-was.html.

Chapter 7

Worldometers. 2025. "Abortions." Accessed March 26. https://www.worldometers.info/abortions/.

Oldest.org. 2025. "8 Youngest Premature Baby to Survive in History." Accessed March 26. https://www.oldest.org/people/youngest-premature-baby-to-survive/.

Cleveland Clinic. 2022. "Progesterone." Cleveland Clinic, December 29. https://my.clevelandclinic.org/health/body/24562-progesterone.

Feltman, Rachel, Hannah Seo, Fonda Mwangi, and Alex Sugiura. 2025. "This Hormone-Free Pill Could Finally Expand Birth Control Options for Men." *Scientific American* Podcast, August 13. https://www. scientificamerican.com/podcast/episode/a-male-birth-control-pill-moves-to-the-next-clinical-trial-stage/.

World Population Review. 2025. "Abortions Due to Rape by State 2025." Accessed March 26. https://worldpopulationreview.com/state-rankings/abortions-due-to-rape-by-state.

Chapter 8

Jones, Rachel, and Jenna Jerman. 2017. "Abortion Is a Common Experience for U.S. Women, Despite Dramatic Declines in Rates." Guttmacher Institute, October 19. https://www.guttmacher.org/news-release/2017/abortion-common-experience-us-women-despite-dramatic-declines-rates.

Diamant, Jeff, Besheer Mohamed, and Rebecca Leppert. 2024. "What the Data Says About Abortion in the U.S." Pew Research Center, March 25. https://www.pewresearch.org/short-reads/2024/03/25/what-the-data-says-about-abortion-in-the-us/.

Chapter 9

The Life Institute. 2022. "Abortion Survivor: Josiah's Story." The Life Institute, January 21. https://thelifeinstitute.net/learning-centre/personal-stories/abortion-survivor-josiahs-story#.

Bilger, Micaiah. 2019. "Teen Who Lost His Legs in Botched Abortion Became a Champion Wrestler." LifeNews, November 12. https://www.lifenews.com/2019/11/12/teen-who-lost-his-legs-in-botched-abortion-became-a-champion-wrestler/.

Eley, Abigail, and Jason Adnitt. 2018. "The Failed Abortion Survivor Whose Mum Thought She Was Dead." BBC News, June 4. https://www.bbc.com/news/health-44357373.

Deaton, Todd. 2022. "A Life Conceived Through Rape Still Worth Saving." *The Baptist Courier*, January 7. https://baptistcourier.com/2022/01/a-life-conceived-through-rape-still-worth-saving/.

Chapter 10

Gaitan, Elyse, Mia Steupert, and Tessa Cox. 2024. "Fact Sheet: Reasons for Abortion." Charlotte Lozier Institute, May 24. https://lozierinstitute.org/fact-sheet-reasons-for-abortion/.

Robertson, Rachael. 2024. "6 Medical Reasons for Abortion." *Everyday Health*, December 19. Accessed March 27, 2025. https://www.everydayhealth.com/abortion/scenarios-where-abortion-can-be-life-saving/.

Tommy's. 2023. "Terminating a Pregnancy for Medical Reasons (TFMR)." Tommy's, May 25,. Accessed March 27, 2025. https://www.tommys.org/baby-loss-support/tfmr-terminating-pregnancy-medical-reasons.

Flanders, Nancy. 2023. "Told that she and her baby would both likely die, she still refused abortion." *LiveAction*. https://www.liveaction.org/news/told-life-risk-baby-die-refused-abortion

Gordoni, Michaela. 2025. "'The Greatest Miracle': Tim Tebow Shares His Pro-Life Birth Story." Movieguide, April 24. Accessed March 27, 2025. https://www.movieguide.org/news-articles/the-greatest-miracle-tim-tebow-shares-his-pro-life-birth-story.html.

Nickvujicic.com. 2025. Accessed April 27. https://nickvujicic.com/.

Chapter 11

Coleman, Priscilla K. 2011. "Abortion and Mental Health: Quantitative Synthesis and Analysis of Research Published 1995–2009." *The British Journal of Psychiatry* 199 (3): 180–186. https://pubmed.ncbi.nlm.nih.gov/21881096/.

Chapter 12

Durkan-Simonds, Deirdre. 2023. "Celebrities Who Waited Until Marriage to Have Sex." *Daily Mail*, November 19. https://www.dailymail.co.uk/tvshowbiz/article-12755597/celebrities-waited-marriage-sex.html.

Chang, Mahalia. 2020. "23 Celebrities Who Waited Until Marriage: No, It's Not Just Justin and Hailey." *Elle Australia*, May 18. https://www.elle.com.au/culture/celebrity/celebrities-who-waited-until-marriage-for-sex-19828/.

DiDonato, Theresa. 2021. "Are Couples That Live Together Before Marriage More Likely to Divorce? Times Have Changed, but Maybe Not Completely." *Psychology Today*, January 27. Accessed March 27, 2025. https://www.psychologytoday.com/us/blog/meet-catch-and-keep/202101/are-couples-that-live-together-before-marriage-more-likely-to.

Warner, Alex. 2019. "35 Celebrities Who Didn't Have Sex Before Marriage." *Marie Claire*, February 14. https://www.marieclaire.com/culture/g19792227/celebrities-that-didnt-have-sex-before-marriage/.

Chapter 13

Christian Life Resources. 2018. "The Abortion Pill and the Morning-After Pill: Are They the Same?" Christian Life Resources, May 4. https://christianliferesources.com/2018/05/04/the-abortion-pill-and-the-morning-after-pill-are-they-the-same/.

Chapter 14

Lerner, Richard. 2000. National Survey of Family Growth. Chicago: University of Chicago.

Wright, Paul J., Ryann S. Tokunaga, and Ashley Kraus. 2016. "A Meta-Analysis of Pornography Consumption and Its Impact on Sexual Aggression and Attitudes Toward Women." *Journal of Communication* 66 (1): 183–205. https://doi.org/10.1111/jcom.12220.

Doe, Jane, and Andrew Smith. 2007. "Effectiveness of Modern Natural Family Planning Methods." Human Reproduction 22 (4): 987–993. https://doi.org/10.1093/humrep/dem123.

Pope Paul VI. 1968. Humanae Vitae. Vatican City: Libreria Editrice Vaticana.

Centers for Disease Control and Prevention (CDC). 2025. "Abortion Surveillance – United States, 1990." Accessed March 27. https://www.cdc.gov/abortion/surveillance/1990.

Chapter 15

Paine, Amy L., Oliver Perra, Rebecca Anthony, and Katherine H. Shelton. 2021. "Charting the Trajectories of Adopted Children's Emotional and Behavioral Problems: The Impact of Early Adversity and Postadoptive Parental Warmth." *Development and Psychopathology* 33 (3): 922–936 https://www.ncbi.nlm.nih.gov/pmc/articles/PMC8374623/.

Tapestry Adoptions. 2025. "How Do Children Feel About Being Adopted?" Tapestry Adoptions Blog, July 16. https://tapestry-adoption.com/how-do-children-feel-about-being-adopted/.

Dave Thomas Foundation for Adoption. 2025. Home page. Dave Thomas Foundation for Adoption. Accessed August 30. https://www. davethomasfoundation.org/.

American Pregnancy Association. "Open Adoption: Advantages and Benefits." Accessed March 27, 2025. https://americanpregnancy.org/ child-adoption/open-adoption-advantages/.

Chapter 16

Baumeister, Roy F., Kathleen D. Vohs, and Jennifer L. Aaker. 2013. "Some Key Differences between a Happy Life and a Meaningful Life." Psychological Science 24 (1): 30–37. https://doi. org/10.1177/0956797612451221.

Brotto, Lori A., Rodney Basson, and Melissa Luria. 2012. "A Mindfulness-Based Group Psychoeducational Intervention Targeting Sexual Arousal Disorder in Women." *Journal of Sexual Medicine* 9 (3): 803–817. https://doi.org/10.1111/j.1743-6109.2011.02605.x.

Chatzittofis, Athanasios, Stefan Arver, Karin Oberg, Johan Hallberg, and Per Nordström. 2016. "Testosterone, Gonadotropins, and Emotional Distress in Compulsive Sexual Behavior." *Journal of Sexual Medicine* 13 (4): 627–636. https://doi.org/10.1016/j.jsxm.2016.01.013.

Dhuffar, Maharaj K., and Mark D. Griffiths. 2014. "Understanding the Role of Loneliness in Sexual Addiction." *Psychology Research and Behavior Management* 7: 25–35. https://doi.org/10.2147/PRBM. S50868.

Hall, Kathryn S., Caroline Moreau, James Trussell, and Jacqueline Barber. 2019. "Determinants of Sexual Boundaries and Their Impact on Well-Being: A Review of Recent Research." *Contraception*: 1–10. https://doi.org/10.1016/j.contraception.2018.10.012.

Kraus, Shane W., Steven Martino, and Marc N. Potenza. 2016. "Clinical Characteristics of Men Interested in Seeking Treatment for Use of Pornography." *Journal of Behavioral Addictions* 5 (2): 169–178. https://doi.org/10.1556/2006.5.2016.036.

Reid, Rory C., Sari Garos, and T. Fong. 2012. "Psychometric Development of the Hypersexual Behavior Consequences Scale." Journal of Sex and Marital Therapy 38 (1): 30–51. https://doi.org/10.1080/00 92623X.2012.643879.

Chapter 17

Gallup International. 2023. "More Prone to Believe in God than Identify as Religious. More Likely to Believe in Heaven than in Hell." Last modified December 4. https://gallup-international.com/survey-results-and-news/survey-result/more-prone-to-believe-in-god-than-identify-as-religious-more-likely-to-believe-in-heaven-than-in-hell.

World Health Organization. 2013. Global and Regional Estimates of Violence against Women: Prevalence and Health Effects of Intimate Partner Violence and Non-Partner Sexual Violence. Geneva: World Health Organization.

Cantor, James M., Steven Martino, Stefano Tripodi, and William Rinn. 2008. "Neuroanatomical Correlates of Pedophilic Disorder: A Voxel-Based Morphometric Study." *Journal of Sexual Medicine* 5 (5): 1101–1112.

Rape, Abuse & Incest National Network (RAINN). 2025. "Effects of Sexual Violence." Accessed July 31. https://rainn.org/effects-sexual-violence.

O'Donnell, Brenna. 2021. "Rise in Online Enticement and Other Trends: NCMEC Releases 2020 Exploitation Stats." Missing Kids, February 24. https://www.missingkids.org/blog/2021/rise-in-online-enticement-and-other-trends--ncmec-releases-2020-.

Whealin, Julia, PhD, and Erin Barnett, PhD. 2025. "Child Sexual Abuse." U.S. Department of Veterans Affairs – National Center for PTSD. Last updated March 25. https://www.ptsd.va.gov/professional/treat/type/sexual_abuse_child.

American Psychiatric Association. 2013. *Diagnostic and Statistical Manual of Mental Disorders. 5th ed.* Arlington, VA: American Psychiatric Association.

Chapter 18

Banks, Duren, and Tracey Kyckelhahn. 2011. Characteristics of Suspected Human Trafficking Incidents, 2008–2010. Washington, DC: Bureau of Justice Statistics, April.

Novotney, Amy. 2023. "7 in 10 Human Trafficking Victims Are Women and Girls: What Are the Psychological Effects?" American Psychological Association, April 24. https://www.apa.org/topics/women-girls/trafficking-women-girls.

Weiss, Rick. 2021. "Love and Sex in the Digital Age: Pornography, Porn-Induced Erectile Dysfunction, Can Pornography Impact Male Sexual Performance?" *Psychology Today*, April 26. https://www.psychologytoday.com/us/blog/love-and-sex-in-the-digital-age/202104/porn-induced-erectile-dysfunction.

Chandra, Anita, Steven C. Martino, Rebecca L. Collins, Marc N. Elliott, Sandra H. Berry, David E. Kanouse, and Angela Miu. 2008. "Exposure to Sex on TV May Increase the Chance of Teen Pregnancy." RAND Corporation Research Brief RB-9398, November 3. https://www.rand.org/pubs/research_briefs/RB9398.html.

Finkelhor, David, Samantha Sutton, Heather Turner & Deirdre Colburn. 2024. "How Risky is Online Sexting by Minors?" *Journal of Child Sexual Abuse* (March 8). DOI: 10.1080/10538712.2024.2324838

Chapter 19

Shafique, Saima, Amna Umer, Kim E. Innes, Toni M. Rudisill, Wei Fang, and Lesley Cottrell. 2022. "Preconception Substance Use and Risk of Unintended Pregnancy: Pregnancy Risk Assessment Monitoring System 2016–17." *Journal of Addiction Medicine* 16 (3): 278–85. https://pubmed.ncbi.nlm.nih.gov/34334685/

National Institute on Alcohol Abuse and Alcoholism. 2016. Alcohol and Intimate Partner Violence. Bethesda, MD: NIAAA, November. http://pubs.niaaa.nih.gov/publications/Social/Module8Intimate-PartnerViolence/Module8.pdf.

Abbey, Antonia. 2011. "Alcohol's Role in Sexual Violence Perpetration: Theoretical Explanations, Existing Evidence, and Future Directions." *Drug and Alcohol Review* 30 (5): 481–89. https://doi.org/10.1111/j.1465-3362.2011.00296.x.

Centers for Disease Control and Prevention (CDC). 2024. "Facts about Excessive Drinking." U.S. Department of Health & Human Services, October 7. https://www.cdc.gov/drink-less-be-your-best/facts-about-excessive-drinking/index.html.

Savin, Jennifer, Jade Biggs, and Sophie Williams. "39 Sober Celebrities Who Say Quitting Alcohol Changed Their Lives." Cosmopolitan, April 24, 2025. https://www.cosmopolitan.com/entertainment/celebs/g64580876/sober-celebrities/

Singh, Olivia. "41 Celebrities Who Have Been Open About Their Sobriety." Business Insider, May 22, 2025. https://www.businessinsider.com/sober-celebrities-who-dont-drink-do-drugs?op=1

Chapter 20

Brewer, Jack. 2023. "Fatherlessness and Its Effects on American Society." Issue brief, America First Policy Institute, May 15. https://www.americafirstpolicy.com/issues/issue-brief-fatherlessness-and-its-effects-on-american-society.

Byers, Melissa. 2021. "The Father Absence Crisis [Infographic]." National Fatherhood Initiative, November 10. https://www.fatherhood.org/championing-fatherhood/the-father-absence-crisis-infographic.

Zill, Nicholas, and Brad Wilcox. 2018. "1 in 2: A New Estimate of the Share of Children Being Raised by Married Parents." Institute for Family Studies, February 27. https://ifstudies.org/blog/1-in-2-a-new-estimate-of-the-share-of-children-being-raised-by-married-parents.

U.S. Bureau of Labor Statistics. 2023. "Education Pays." Career Outlook. https://www.bls.gov/careeroutlook/2023/data-on-display/education-pays.htm.

Pew Research Center. 2019. "Religion's Relationship to Happiness, Civic Engagement and Health Around the World." January 31. https://www.pewresearch.org/religion/2019/01/31/religions-relationship-to-happiness-civic-engagement-and-health-around-the-world/.

World Health Organization. 2025. Promoting Gender Equality to Prevent Violence against Women. Geneva: WHO, accessed August 4. https://iris.who.int/bitstream/handle/10665/44098/9789241597883_eng.pdf.

Sons to Men. 2025. "Building Strong Men, Families, and Communities." Accessed August 4. https://www.sonstomen.org.

Chapter 21

Wilcox, Brad. 2019. "Marriage Facilitates Responsible Fatherhood." Institute for Family Studies, June 12. https://ifstudies.org/blog/marriage-facilitates-responsible-fatherhood.

National Center for Education Statistics. 2024. "Fast Facts: Degrees Conferred by Race/Ethnicity and Sex." NCES, May. https://nces.ed.gov/programs/coe/indicator/cta.

Pew Research Center. "Religion and Happiness Around the World." Religion & Public Life, January 31, 2019. https://www.pewresearch.org/religion/2019/01/31/religions-relationship-to-happiness-civic-engagement-and-health-around-the-world/.

Guttmacher Institute. 2019. "Unintended Pregnancy in the United States." Fact sheet, January. https://www.guttmacher.org/sites/default/files/factsheet/fb-unintended-pregnancy-us.pdf.

Chapter 23

Centers for Disease Control and Prevention (CDC). 2024. "U.S. Pregnancy Rates Drop during Last Decade." April 12, 2023. https://www.cdc.gov/nchs/pressroom/nchs_press_releases/2023/20230412.htm.

Guttmacher Institute. 2019.v"Unintended Pregnancy in the United States." Fact sheet, April. https://www.guttmacher.org/fact-sheet/unintended-pregnancy-united-states.

World Health Organization. 2019. "High Rates of Unintended Pregnancies Linked to Gaps in Family Planning Services." October 25. https://www.who.int/news/item/25-10-2019-high-rates-of-unintended-pregnancies-linked-to-gaps-in-family-planning-services-new-who-study.

Bearak, Jonathan, Anna Popinchalk, Bela Ganatra, et al. 2018. "Unintended Pregnancy and Induced Abortion Worldwide." The Lancet Global Health 6 (11): e1116–e1124.

Duke-Ellis, Sarah, and Jennifer F. Peipert. 2012. "Access to Free Birth Control Reduces Abortion Rates." WashU Medicine News, Oct. 12. https://medicine.wustl.edu/news/access-to-free-birth-control-reduces-abortion-rates.

Mostafavi, Beata. 2020. "Expanded Birth Control Coverage May Help Reduce Disparities in Unplanned Pregnancies." Michigan Medicine, November 6. https://www.michiganmedicine.org/health-lab/expanded-birth-control-coverage-may-help-reduce-disparities-unplanned-pregnancies.

New York State Bipartisan Pro-Choice Legislative Caucus. 2025. "Sex Education." Accessed June. https://www.nysbpclc.com/sex-education.html.

Masserly, Megan. 2023. "Sex Ed, Birth Control, Medicaid: Republicans' 'New Pro-Life Agenda.'" Politico, March 30. https://www.politico.com/news/2023/03/30/gop-pro-life-agenda-00089550.

Williams, Diane Duke. 2012. "Access to Free Birth Control Reduces Abortion Rates." Washington University School of Medicine News, October 12. https://medicine.washu.edu/news/access-to-free-birth-control-reduces-abortion-rates.

Abortionworker.com. 2025. Accessed June 1. https://www.abortionworker.com.

Gaul, Moira. 2015. "Pregnancy Help Centers More Likely to be Welcomed into Neighborhoods Than Planned Parenthood." Charlotte Lozier Institute, August 4. https://lozierinstitute.org/pregnancy-help-centers-more-likely-to-be-welcomed-into-neighborhoods-than-planned-parenthood/.

Arnett, Jeffrey J. 2000. "Emerging Adulthood: A Theory of Development from the Late Teens through the Twenties." American Psychologist 55 (5): 469–480. https://doi.org/10.1037/0003-066X.55.5.469.

Barlow, Ellen. 2014. "Under the Hood of the Adolescent Brain." Center on the Developing Child at Harvard University, October 17. https://clbb.mgh.harvard.edu/under-the-hood-of-the-adolescent-brain/.

Divorce.com. 2024. "U.S. Divorce Rate: 51+ Essential Statistics." July 15. https://divorce.com/blog/divorce-statistics/.

Zheng, Chi, and Ying Wu. 2019. "The More Modest You Are, the Happier You Are: The Mediating Roles of Emotional Intelligence and Self-Esteem." *Journal of Happiness Studies* 20, (5): 1509–1523. https://doi.org/10.1007/s10902-018-9984-4.

Zheng, C., Wu, Q., Jin, Y., et al. 2017. "Regional gray matter volume is associated with trait modesty: Evidence from voxel-based morphometry." *Scientific Reports*, 7(1). 1–9.

Stanley, Andy. *The New Rules for Love, Sex, and Dating*. Grand Rapids, MI: Zondervan, 2015.

Behrendt, Greg, and Liz Tuccillo. *He's Just Not That Into You*. New York: Simon Spotlight Entertainment, 2004.

Behrendt, Greg and Amiira Ruotola-Behrendt. *It's Called a Breakup Because It's Broken: The Smart Girl's Breakup Buddy*. New York: Broadway Books, 2005.